Bauman's Legacy

Bauman's Legacy

A Critical Analysis on the Crisis of Modernity

Carlo Bordoni

ANTHEM PRESS

Anthem Press
An imprint of Wimbledon Publishing Company
www.anthempress.com

This edition first published in UK and USA 2025
by ANTHEM PRESS
75–76 Blackfriars Road, London SE1 8HA, UK
or PO Box 9779, London SW19 7ZG, UK
and
244 Madison Ave #116, New York, NY 10016, USA

British Library Cataloguing-in-Publication Data
A catalogue record for this book is available from the British Library.

Library of Congress Cataloging-in-Publication Data: 2024952839
A catalog record for this book has been requested.

ISBN-13: 978-1-83999-497-5 (Pbk)
ISBN-10: 1-83999-497-5 (Pbk)

Cover image: Giampaolo Prampolini
Cover design: Mauro Cremonini

This title is also available as an e-book.

CONTENTS

INTRODUCTION

Was not modernity a process
of 'liquefaction' from the start?
Was not 'melting the solids' its major pastime
and prime accomplishment all along?
In other words, has modernity
not been 'fluid' since its inception?

Liquid Modernity, 2000: 2–3.

What remains of the idea of liquid modernity? Is Bauman's thought still relevant? This volume aims to answer these questions, offering an analysis of his work, starting from the theorization of liquid society. Without forgetting the vastness and complexity of his work, where the idea of liquidity remains fundamental, but not unique, before and after the central turning point of the year 2000.

There are two cornerstones that must be adhered to in order to understand the development of critical thought in our time: Max Weber and Bauman himself. He can only be compared to Weber in terms of the originality and social impact of his work in the identical field of the analysis of modern society: the one opens up the discourse on modernity at the beginning of the twentieth century, with his deep analysis of religions and their socio-economic impact, while the other closes the century, with his attempt to safeguard what remains of the *Neuzeit* in a sustainable, albeit liquefied condition. All this in the aftermath of the tragedies and upheavals that have in the meantime swept through the Western world and that seem to give reason to what Oswald Spengler, just a century ago, predicted about the inevitable decline of our civilization.

More likely, unlike Spengler's pessimistic vision, it is modernity, and not Western civilization, that has entered into an acute crisis of values. The spirit in which the great proponents of the "new time"—from Jean Bodin to Thomas Hobbes, from Jean-Jacques Rousseau to Montesquieu—were born has been misrepresented and even neglected, allowing the great expectations and promises of the origins to be dropped.

Bauman was perfectly aware of this, and his search for truth never ceased, right up to the end, to urge us to understand, to put us in a position to choose for the future, narrating—as a privileged observer—his experience as a man who spanned the entire twentieth century, with its illusions and disappointments, sufferings and hopes. From Communism to Zionism, from the holocaust to the resurgence of reactionary movements—he had been greatly affected by the protests of neo-Nazi groups received during his last visit to Poland, where they had publicly burnt his image—he was a witness of the century, personally involved.

But in the project of modernity, he still believed and believed that after this phase of crisis—an interregnum in which there is a momentary lawlessness ("a time when the old ways of doing things no longer work properly, but in which new and more effective ways are not yet available," Bauman recalls, quoting Gramsci)—the path of civilization would resume its course with serenity and confidence.

Bauman was an optimist; he believed in humanity and its possibility of redemption. That is why liquidity should be seen as an accident along the way, an obstacle on the road to progress, or rather a necessary step to reset the social order and start again from the beginning.

If we limit Bauman's contribution to the theorization of liquid modernity, we risk a *deminutio*, a reductionism that impedes understanding: his is a strenuous and passionate defense of the ideals of freedom, solidarity, responsibility, progress, democracy, and equality at a time when these qualities seem to be called into question by an excessive individualism, intent only on defending itself and surviving even at the expense of others. An individualism that has formed a mistaken idea of freedom and appears disappointed by the expectations of progress.

Social Responsibilities

Bauman's legacy is multiform and complex, subdivided into partial legacies, not all of which are homogeneous and acceptable without the benefit of inventory. The first difficulty consists in its complete lack of systematicity: Bauman-thought is by no means a single whole, nor can it be used as a key instrument to be applied to every condition, given that it explicitly concerns a precise fraction of our present. This is not to be understood as an oversight, but a conscious, strongly-intended choice to eschew any systematic, systematizing formulation of society. He prefers to understand the sociologist's task as an acute observer, capable of enabling social agents—i.e., all human beings—to make the right choices with awareness of its risks, as well as its effects.

He has been unfairly accused of not conducting field research, those quantitative investigations that gather data and statistics, on the basis of which one can offer scientific and incontrovertible demonstrations of an effected reality. Instead, Bauman suspects that sometimes quantitative data are misleading and do not always offer an objective representation of the truth, which remains hidden and needs an interpretative effort. Therefore, it needs to be unveiled. An exegetical process that goes beyond appearances. Intellectuals were once legislators and interpreters, and since the task of legislating has been taken away from them, the task of interpreters remains fundamental. This is the primary duty of the sociologist. A qualitative task that, regardless of the available data, must not be limited to the simple exposition of apparent reality.

Bauman's legacy leaves a bitter taste in the mouth, since in its very concluding phase it reveals pessimistic implications that seem to contradict his previous positions, so full of hope and confidence in the opportunities for improvement of humans. The very theorization of liquidity itself seemed to suggest, in the peaceful understanding of a phase of disorientation, the possibility of rediscovering momentarily forgotten human values, first and foremost social solidarity, a purely modern aspect that refers to Marx, class relations, and class consciousness. Solidarity is indicated as the *conditio sine qua non* for a society to be defined as such.

Keeping this in mind, in addition to Marx, the teaching of Emmanuel Lévinas, according to which everyone is responsible for the other. The invitation to overcome exasperated individualism, the latest and most recent expression of subjectivism, is constant in Bauman, but it can only be seen as an ethical requirement, on which—as in the case of the conspicuous wealth of which Veblen speaks—his strenuous opposition to any existential drift hinges.

If All That Is Solid Melts Into Air

As Marx wrote, echoed by Marshall Berman in his most famous essay, "All that is solid melts into air, all that is holy is profaned" (*The Communist Manifesto*, 1848). It is almost an anticipation of the concept of liquidity, which comes to Bauman through Berman. Indeed, it is likely that Bauman owes something to Berman, where the concept of solid modernity begins to be questioned. Although there is no doubt about Marx's influence; Peter Beilharz suggests that "an absent presence in Bauman's writing was the figure and work of Marshall Berman, specifically in *All that is Solid Melts into Air. The Experience of Modernity* (1982); is itself a ubiquitous presence, a talisman, and almost a sacred cow for contemporary cultural studies of the period. Marx was, for Berman, the perfect figure of modernity and modernism, where ambivalence, ambition, and enthusiasm for these social forms spilled over into each other. Berman's task was to try to hold these tensions together so that the modern retained its sense of promise, as well as its sense of threat" (Beilharz 2000: 60).

It should not be forgotten that the bourgeoisie of which Marx speaks is not exactly the middle class, which instead represents its largest and lowest fraction. The ever-increasing gap between the middle and upper middle classes, and the diversity of their interests and expectations, will soon lead to a deep fracture between the two incompatible components of the bourgeois class, until the constitution of a new social composition, the mass, of an interclass character, where a multiplicity of components (including the underclass and the marginalized) will converge, with the exclusion of the upper bourgeois fraction, which will instead constitute the hegemonic elite.

We are in the midst of postmodernity, it should not be forgotten, and the feeling that the mighty construction put up for three centuries is destined to crumble makes our ears perk up, alarms us, and leads us to reflect on those who, like Bauman, already have doubts about the development that has occurred since the Industrial Revolution, through social struggles, positivism, and the birth of mass society. What is more, questioned by another social critic significant for his influence on Bauman himself, i.e., Ulrich Beck (1986) who theorizes a society of risk and even a second or third modernity. Yet in the 1990s, when Bauman was writing these texts, the signs were already loud and clear. Jeremy Rifkin (1995) pointed to an imminent end of work, André Gorz (1988) saw in the immaterial labor the future of the world economy, while Francis Fukuyama (1992) even predicted an end of history. Globalization was already a reality and called into question the stability of jobs for millions of people. Behind all this was the rapid technological evolution, which was becoming increasingly difficult to keep up with and which was beyond the control of humanity forced to suffer its economic and cultural impacts. The personal computer and the network had already made their overbearing entrance into people's lives, they were no longer just complex working tools for large companies but were becoming everyday objects for private individuals, changing the way they communicated, learned, worked, and enjoyed themselves. Behind this was another serious crisis, perhaps less obvious, but no less decisive for the society that was experiencing it with a sort of ill-concealed complacency: the crisis of modernity.

Crisis and New Technologies

The very sense of the uniqueness of modernity is questioned as Shmuel Eisenstadt (2002) speaks of *multiple modernities* that have had different times and developments in different locations around the world. The very idea of a single modernity, the true "discrete object" of our history, is thus questioned, fragmented, and separated in its substantive lines. The deconstruction of the modern, started by Jacques Derrida, in the wake of Martin Heidegger, and before him by Friedrich Nietzsche (to mention only the main interlocutors of the affirmation/primacy of subjectivity), cannot but find disagreement with those who, like Bauman, see in Marx, along with Berman, the reference exponent of modern sensibility. All this on condition that we take note of the transience of earthly matters and that, therefore, all that is solid is not meant to last forever.

In this climate of creeping and unstoppable degradation, the revision of modernity in liquid form was ingenious and decisive (at least temporarily), since on the one hand, it saved what could be saved, while on the other, it confronted the supporters of subjectivism with the dialectically inescapable possibility of another option besides that of an irrational nihilism, devoid of any concrete perspective other than that of a regress of civilization. As he has observed on many occasions, the introduction of new technologies and, in particular, of the Internet, has led to an easier and more intuitive realization of social relations in those platforms which, not by chance, are called "social," but which have very little that is social about them.

Not only for their precarity—Bauman points out how easy it is, with a single click, to cancel a relationship and end a friendship—but above all for the essence of any form of solidarity. On the contrary, the anonymity, distance, and type of the medium itself invite rather to self-promotion, the manifestation of the self, the spectacularization of one's private life, if not even aggression towards the other. Haters are in fact a new and worryingly growing phenomenon, as they increase isolation, foment hatred, and end up further restricting social relations. We are moving towards a society that is increasingly made up of lonely, dissatisfied people, unable to maintain social relationships worthy of the name and therefore very little inclined to solidarity.

The Time of Late Style

The late style of Bauman, in the sense that Peter Beilharz attributes to him, seems especially evident in the very last works, from *State of Crisis* (2014a) to *Retrotopia* (2017a), where repetitions of the same concepts and the reworking in didactic form of previous statements prevail over new formulations. There is a certain weariness, but also a stubborn consistency with the previous formulas: not only the concept of liquidity, reaffirmed and radicalized in the new *Preface* to *Liquid Modernity* in 2011, but also in the refrains on the divorce between power and politics, the rejection of multiculturalism, postmodernism, and the mantra on the need for local solutions to local problems.

The idea of utopia as a product of modernity remains relevant: "Utopia— he wrote in *Socialism, Active Utopia* (1976a)—is an absolutely modern phenomenon." Utopia is part of the new time that revolutionizes the past and makes one look to the future with a positive and progressive spirit.

Bauman is the last great sociologist of modernity: *Retrotopia* is its epilogue, as it closes a time, and puts an end to the attempt to safeguard modernity, albeit in its liquefied form. It is not only the end of utopia—in Dahrendorf's sense (1968)—but the end of a century, the twentieth century, characterized by frustrated hopes and disappointments, in which all the principles that had made modernity a powerful factor of development and a reservoir of certainties have disappeared: faith in science, progress, ideologies, and even social education, the last legacy of Rousseau's pedagogical idea, expressed in *Emile or Education* (1762), which totalitarianism have instrumentalized and taken to its extreme (and tragic) consequences in their attempt to assume absolute control of the masses. But also the end of the conception of the modern state, the collapse of the hopes for equality, democracy, and liberation from need, which had inflamed the social struggles of the second half of the nineteenth century and which had become the cornerstones of the new narratives of progressive thought.

Bauman's attempt to maintain what was valid in modernity, to keep it on its feet through the shrewdness of liquidity, is extinguished in the admission of an interregnum that looks more like a "wasteland" than a laboratory for the cultivation of utopia, whose main prerogative, hope, seems destined to be postponed in time. This is why Bauman's last work, *Retrotopia*, published posthumously, is an act of hope, of a desperate return to the past: a past so distant as to be free of all forms of nostalgia.

A past that can be identified in a very precise time, before the rise of modernity, around the seventeenth century. A time when uncertainty reigned, the state did not yet exist, and fear, the oldest feeling in the world, guided men's actions. There is something sarcastic in the postponement to that crucial moment, when everything still had to happen and choices had not yet been made; when the multitudes—the ensemble of peoples, in Spinoza's definition—were not yet a people.

No Voluntary Servitude

Bauman, with his fluid vision of contemporary society, has characterized the beginning of the third millennium, showing its uncertainties, fears, and existential insecurities. The idea of liquidity, which dates back to the end of the 1990s and is now measured by an existence of almost twenty years, in its stabilization does not free the global citizen from loneliness, nor does it entail overcoming the crisis, but covers everything with an impalpable veil. Liquidity made gelatinous, impregnating, viscous, in the now inescapable awareness of a waiting condition that it is impossible to know how long it will last.

With Bauman also goes an original sociological methodology, far removed from any academicism; with his passing, we can truly speak of the end of the liquid world, as it is essentially linked to his extraordinary capacity for analysis. His thought marked an era, that of uncertainty and precariousness, which followed the ephemeral enthusiasms of post-modernism. The definition of liquid modernity immediately imposed itself as the most suitable one to represent a time of crisis; it has resisted the assaults of official critics, the criticisms of detractors, and the solicitations of those who, like Ulrich Beck, proposed the assumption of a second or even third modernity, leaving the dialogue open.

The only permissible dialogue, according to Bauman, was that between people who do not think alike, but whose interaction is productive of new meaning. He branded any attempt at complacency as an example of "voluntary servitude" (quoting Étienne de la Boétie). He was a master in this too. In the most difficult art of teaching without demanding passive acceptance of his opinions. And it was precisely on modernity and its decline, in an attempt to adapt it to the Gramscian condition of "interregnum"—of which Bauman himself had made himself the interpreter—that our dialogue ("catalyst of ideas," he used to call it) centered; sometimes in presence, sometimes at a distance or even on the pages of a book with two voices (*State of Crisis*, 2014a).

A Baumanian exception of dialogue had, however, revealed itself in the same correspondence during the writing of *Interregnum. Beyond Liquid Modernity* (2016), where I argued for the idea of the end of modernity.

The publisher had asked him to write an introductory text that could start one of those now rare cultural debates capable of producing a virtuous circle. Unfortunately, the provocation around overcoming liquid society could not be answered, but—as you will read in these pages—the contiguity between the two positions remains much stronger than their diversity.

An interrupted, but by no means withered dialogue, which continues with the analysis of his work. We can then speak more of an evolution than an opposition, according to the same principles that inform Bauman's thought, so adaptable, versatile, and, in a Weberian sense, also comprehensible.

The discussion around the persistence of modernity, however, does not erase the value of the brilliant intuition of a liquid world, which remains the indelible sign of a time; an adjective that has even been abused and vulgarized, but which now more than ever needs to be historicized and framed in the broader context of a middle age, which extends beyond the limits of several generations and which takes on structural connotations that will be difficult to get rid of.

A Still Liquid Society?

So, what remains of the liquid world? What remains of the great theorization constructed by Bauman twenty-five years ago?

The answer is complex since the normal social evolution that has taken place in the meantime has been followed by the pandemic emergency. With the inevitable repercussions on social behavior. Examining the effects that change has produced in the public and private spheres, an almost dystopian world now emerges, far removed from liquidity, where negative tendencies risk being exacerbated.

Very little remains of the liquid world, yet liquidity has had its importance because it is at the origin of change: we cannot understand the current conditions, let alone those that we will experience in the near future, if we do not take into account the drift that began at the turn of the last century, which took root with the economic crisis of 2008, to the point that the current condition can be defined as "post-social," with its deformation of social relations, distinguishing it from the liquid-modern world, which preceded it. As a change without return, liquidity should be seen as a negative development of the solid-modern structure. Indeed, it is from liquidity that the process of destroying social ties begins. First, we witnessed the emergence of individualism, i.e. an increased focus on the rights and autonomy of the individual over the collective. This trend manifested itself as a result of the exit from mass society, accompanied by the end of ideologies, the decline of progressive ideas, and the advance of new economic processes such as neo-liberalism.

The economic crisis, without a solid social support network, where people were left alone to face problems of survival, increased the feeling of uncertainty. It added to the climate of insecurity, which was felt due to a combination of factors ranging from the difficulties of politics (Bauman had already denounced the divorce between power and politics) to the mediatization of relations through technology.

Liquefaction was ultimately the last stroke of modernity's tail, its extreme attempt to resist under the blows of an unstoppable social change, where all the modern cornerstones were gradually being torn down or rendered ineffective. It is as if, over the years, liquidity had congealed, solidified, and hardened; rendered incapable of describing the new forms of life that were pressing in, leaving us in a condition of anxious waiting, what has been called an interregnum. A solidarity that has expressed itself in immunization, a mass operation from which a return to the principles proper to the community transpires. But not of society, if we see it as an evolution of close cooperation, mutual solidarity, and dependence on the other proper to the community.

We are now able to see the limits of liquidity as it surrenders to change. Where even modernity gives way to a new time that has other rules of behavior, no less stringent than the previous ones. Indeed, perhaps more stringent, focusing more on the affirmation of human rather than social characteristics. This is why it can be called "post-society."

In Search of Continuity

This volume brings together a number of texts devoted to the work of Zygmunt Bauman from a critical point of view. In particular, "Sociology from Weber to Bauman" attempts to place his thought in the historical context that sees it at the extreme point of the sociological discourse on modernity, which has developed over a century. Both, Weber and Bauman, represent the high points of a sociology of the modern world, as they best revealed its complexity, innovations, and criticalities: the one when modernity was at its peak, positivist, and progressive; the other when it was now disintegrated and deprived of its solidity. Much of the responsibility for the crisis of modernity, as Bauman himself pointed out in *Modernity and the Holocaust* (1989), can be attributed to the tragic dream of rationalizing and ordering society, just to the inhuman excess of totalitarianism. But secondly, the betrayal of most of the promises of democracy, equality, progress, and freedom.

In the following chapters, the transition from postmodernity to liquid modernity was analyzed ("From Liquid to Solid and Back," "When Bauman was Postmodern"), with the contradictions and insights that characterized his thinking in perpetual adaptation to the changing reality between the end of the twentieth and the beginning of the twenty-first centuries, right up to the introduction of the Gramscian concept of the "interregnum," as an overcoming of certain now unsatisfactory aspects of social liquidity.

"A Praise for Utopia" analyses the importance of utopian thought in Bauman from *Socialism Active Utopia* (1976a), up to the expression of discomfort and disappointment manifested in *Retrotopia*, published posthumously in 2017.

His disappointment is accounted for in "The Multiple Declines of the West," when by then pessimism has erased all hope in the face of escalating conflicts and violence, the resurgence of nationalism and racism. Other chapters dwell on Bauman's biography ("A Life in Fragments," "A Man in a Walk"), on his life as a nomad through the history of the twentieth century, the world war, anti-Semitism, and the move to England. All the way to the "buen retiro" of Lawnswood Gardens, the subject of the book's last text, at the end of a long journey that leaves many questions open. The most disturbing of which is the same: what remains of liquid modernity?

Chapter 1

SOCIOLOGY FROM WEBER TO BAUMAN

The coming century may well be
a time of ultimate catastrophe.
Or it may be a time when a new compact
between intellectuals and the people
—now meaning humanity at large—
is negotiated and brought to life.
Let's hope that the choice between
these two futures are still ours.

Liquid Fear, 2006: 177.

Zygmunt Bauman, the thinker of liquid modernity, has left us an endless amount of books, articles, lectures, notes, and interviews that continue to be published and republished with inexhaustible interest. But the totality of his work cannot be reduced to the idea of liquidity, which was also his happiest insight and one with the most far-reaching media effect. On the contrary, Bauman radically changed the vision of sociology, and sociology has never been the same since his profound operation of reflection and reconstruction according to an innovative vision.

His contribution can be related to that of at least three major exponents of sociological thought, Max Weber, Georg Simmel, and Charles Wright Mills, thus representing an ideal continuity of the development of sociological thought on the libertarian side.

First, Max Weber, the German scholar gave a modern twist to social studies by introducing the principle of "ethical neutrality," or the separation of the observer from the data being analyzed, along with absolute objectivity in examining the results.

His studies tended toward objective and impartial detachment from social analysis, with the aim of maintaining a scientific approach, in the spirit of modern culture proper to the early twentieth century.

Max Weber, for this reason, is considered the sociologist of modernity par excellence, and it is no coincidence that exactly a century later (Weber having lived between the end of the nineteenth century and the 1920s), another sociologist, Zygmunt Bauman, turned the parameters of "neutrality" upside down and made them permeable, conditionable, and flexible. Not by distorting the results of research, but on the contrary by making them more real, adapted to the human condition, less abstract, and, for this reason, more understandable. Bauman closes the circle of the short century of the most exasperated modernity, certainly not by posing himself as "anti-modern" and consequently reactionary, in the wake of anti-modernism from Nietzsche to Heidegger, but by searching in the origins of Enlightenment and utopian modernity for those positive elements necessary for adaptation to social change.

Liquidity, in short, not as the crumbling drift of a solid society, but as modernity's extreme attempt to understand the present: an advanced modernity of more complex and difficult understanding, or even a second modernity, according to another great German scholar who had much in common with Bauman, Ulrich Beck, who passed away in January 2015.

The Loneliness of the Metropolitan Citizen

Georg Simmel is Bauman's other great point of reference when he developed a sociology that deals with all forms of social interaction and researches "modes and forms of sociation": the forms and not the laws of behavior, which cannot be codified or normalized. Human actions cannot be explained, but only observed in their form as spontaneously produced.

Bauman appeals to Simmel for his focus on lived experience, especially taking into account the latter's caution against any attempt to "explain" social behaviors, which can only be observed in their forms (which is why we speak of pure or formal sociology) and interpreted, though without drawing from their rules of behavior to which individuals must adhere.

The universal impossibility of setting rules or predicting behavior is constant in Bauman, who prefers the interpretation of actions to it. His is, as he has repeatedly called it, "sociological hermeneutics":

> My kind of sociology I call *sociological hermeneutics*—he writes in *What Use is Sociology?*—It consists in the interpretation of human choices as manifestations of strategies constructed in response to the challenges of the socially shaped situation and where one has been placed in it. Human choices are no more determined—though no less either—than the moves of card players are determined by the cards in their hand." And finally, "Interpretation (both primary and the secondary) being perpetually *in statu nascendi*, and its finding therefore being barred from claiming a status more solid than that of an interim settlement, a perpetual 'state of crisis' is bound to be sociology's natural habit." (Bauman 2014a: 40, 60)

From Simmel's thought also seems to come the reflection on individual loneliness, which manifests itself—in the absence of a cohesive community—where the group becomes disproportionately large and complex in large cities as a result of urbanization and the division of social labor. The overly large group, as is the case in metropolitan cities, escapes the relational capacity of the individual, who is increasingly driven to isolate himself and recognize in his neighbor or coworker more a potential adversary than a sodal. This is the alienation of the modern citizen, lost within the metropolis, ready to seek superficial and ephemeral contacts in order to satisfy his need to socialize.

The self-enclosure, in addition to fueling selfish behavior, forces the individual to find refuge in autonomous practices or spaces of refuge, where social relations are purely symbolic or virtual. Here, Simmel seems to be preconceiving social and the sublimation of networked communications, which Bauman has timely studied and attributed to the liquefaction of modern society.

A Sociology with Visionary Potential

Bauman radically changed the vision of sociology, which was never the same after his profound operation of reflection and reconstruction according to an innovative vision. The third sociologist of reference for establishing the continuity of Bauman's impact in the sociological perspective can only be the American Charles Wright Mills. A brilliant nonconformist, a professor at Columbia University in New York, who left at the age of only 46 in 1962, Mills is the real missing piece in understanding the long travail suffered by modern sociology in the transition from Weber to Bauman.

Through *The Sociological Imagination* (1959), in fact, Mills identifies the great promise of the social sciences in the possibility for individuals to "understand his own experience and gauge his own fate only by locating himself within his period" thus acquiring a real political awareness and revealing to men and women "the real reasons for their experience, so as to make them politically conscious individuals" (Wright Mills 2000: 5).

Around the middle of the last century—ideally balancing between the two extremes of modernity—Mills finally breaks with a rigid and bureaucratic approach to sociology. That empirical approach that was prevalent in the United States, represented especially by the structural-functionalism of Talcott Parsons, the "great theorizer," accused of abstractness and dullness in the face of real social problems.

Bauman brings to an end the "liberating" project of sociology begun by Mills, making it no longer a means of investigating and perhaps directing society—a task to which certain sociology, at least until the 1960s, had devoted itself with diligence, useful to governments, the strong powers, and the corporations of consumerism. Sociology then becomes a tool for individual knowledge and consciousness-raising, autonomy, and choice-making. An epochal shift, to which is added a marked preference for qualitative analysis, using statistical data only when they are needed to understand social phenomena, never making them the primary object of research. At the center of this sociology are individuals, their personal relationships, and the conditions in which they live, in the historical perspective of their becoming.

After Bauman, sociology will never be the same: it will have to revise its parameters, and seriously ask itself what its goals are. Whether it will intend to remain an ancillary science of power or make itself a means of liberation for the individual, making him aware, politically aware, of his human experience and his opportunities to change the world.

Beyond the liquid world, the last fraction of modernity in crisis lies a completely different reality waiting to be imagined. For only through imagination and the visionary potential of humanity, it is possible to build the future.

The Sociological Evolution

To understand the development of this young science, it is necessary to briefly trace its long journey from Max Weber to Zygmunt Bauman. It was born in France in the second half of the nineteenth century as a result of the political and cultural turmoil of a restless society, where the uprisings of 1848 and the publication of the *Communist Party Manifesto* stirred the crowds and foreshadowed the rise of a new social subject, the mass. An elusive and unpredictable phenomenon, difficult to contain, in need of new tools of understanding and control, which the authorities still lacked.

Added to this are the effects of the introduction of mechanization in production processes and the economic, political, and social upheavals caused by the first Industrial Revolution. Sociology was born concealing within itself an underlying ambiguity, which would remain within it for much of its later development: the need for a rational understanding of the society in which we live and the tendency toward the liberation of man, following the lead of the Enlightenment spirit of the previous century as expressed by one of its precursors, Baron Charles de Montesquieu (1750).

But the official godfather is Auguste Comte, who is credited with having first used the term "sociology" within his *Course in Positive Philosophy* (1830–1842), definitively separating a philosophical conception of society from a more pragmatic and functional one. Influenced by the growing importance of the sciences and technology in nineteenth-century society, sociology emerged, though without precise political aims, as an attempt to study human behavior with the same methodologies employed in physiology and the natural sciences.

The prevailing orientation of social thought in the second half of the nineteenth century, from which sociology emerged as a new discipline which was characterized by the reaction of traditionalism against analytical reason. Paradoxically, sociology, although it finds its constitutive and political reasons in the openings of modernity, stands, as to its perspectives, within a conservative conception.

In this sense, both Auguste Comte and Émile Durkheim look substantially toward the restoration of a disrupted social order, more concerned with maintaining a condition of "normality" through a moral authority that guarantees social control and, in fact, prevents all change, which is considered dangerously negative. Anomie, that is, lawlessness, is indeed a constant in Durkheim's thought.

Later Durkheim, a founding father together with Comte, was concerned with establishing the objectivity of social facts by setting the first "rules of sociological method," but it will be Max Weber who was concerned in the early twentieth century to exclude from this new science any temptation to make value judgments, in the modern spirit of a quest for absolute objectivity, not conditioned by the observer's thinking, nor by a thesis-driven research.

In *The Meaning of "Ethical Neutrality" in Sociology and Economics*, Weber recognizes how "the investigator and teacher should keep unconditionally separate the establishment of empirical facts (including the 'value-oriented' conduct of the empirical individual whom he is investigating) and his own practical evaluations, i.e., his evaluation of these facts as satisfactory or unsatisfactory (including among these facts evaluations made by the empirical persons who are the objects of investigation). These two things are logically different and to deal with them as though they were the same represents a confusion of entirely heterogeneous problems." [...] An investigator can however take his own evaluation as a 'fact' and then draw conclusions from it" (Weber 1949: 11).

Departing from the positivist matrix as an attempt to introduce the scientific method into the study of social relations, sociology thus seeks to free itself from any prejudicial conditioning. Weber can be considered the turning point of modern sociology, the one who determined the approach of research throughout the twentieth century. After him, the developments were manifold, sometimes making this young science a useful instrument of social control, precisely by using the initial claim of "ethical neutrality" (*Wertfreiheit*) and scientific objectivity.

After all, precisely between the early twentieth century and the end of World War II, the most pressing social problem was the masses, and their problematic and uncontrollable participation, which totalitarianism sought to ride and use to their benefit.

A Reactionary Drift

Between the late nineteenth and early twentieth centuries, ideas of collective, social, and democratic participation, became prevalent over the private: the mass emerges, the absolute protagonist of history, and sociology finds here its first and most complex research ground, using the tools it has at its disposal, sometimes overstepping its limits or even bending science to oppressive and liberticidal ends.

In this sense, Cesare Lombroso's "criminal sociology" seeks to trace the signs of abnormal behavior in facial features and skull conformation, corroborating the racist theses of Arthur de Gobineau (1853–1854).

In *Criminal Man* (1876), Lombroso espouses the positivist idea of observing social facts to draw inferences and rules of social behavior but demonstrates how such a schematic and obtuse method can lead to aberrant conclusions. Lombroso was answered by Scipio Sighele with *The Criminal Crowd* (1891), while socialist Filippo Turati overturned Lombroso's thesis in a provocative pamphlet, *The Criminal State* (1883), which shifted the research rather to group behavior, denying the atavistic nature of the propulsion to delinquency.

"Social psychology," a new discipline situated somewhere between sociology and psychoanalysis, seeks to mediate individual problems, on which it tries to shed light with some success, with collective ones, the emergence of which has come to the attention of observers and scholars. At this stage, interventions are mostly aimed at understanding the behavior of the crowd as a negative force. The central issue lies in its dangerousness, the uncontrollable violence it is capable of unleashing, and the search for appropriate means to control it and quell its subversive force. Crowd violence is first considered in the same way as the criminal behavior of the individual, and evaluated as such, to resolve itself in the criminal association, which has an obvious intentionality and makes use of the involvement of more than one person to better achieve its aims.

A Science for Controlling the Masses

In its irrepressible need for "cum-prehension," comprehensive sociology seeks to find an adequate solution to the problem of the masses. It does so through the founding father of modern sociology, the same Max Weber who had argued for the neutrality of science, for objective research, liberated from all instrumental interests.

The spread of faith in science is observed by Weber with concern about the rationalization of social life and the consequent disappearance of the "disenchantment (*Entzauberung*) of the world": "The growing process of intellectualization and rationalization—he writes in *Science as a Vocation* (*Wissenschaft als Beruf*, 1919)—does not imply a growing understanding of the conditions under which we live. [...] it means that principally there are no mysterious incalculable forces that come into play, but rather that one can, in principle, master all things by calculation. This means that the world is disenchanted" (Weber 2004: 12–13).

Thus it is that the development of Western society tends more and more worryingly toward bureaucratic forms that stiffen social structures, endangering personal and intellectual freedom, a value Weber favors above all others. In his studies on the influence of religions on society and, later, in the systematic work that would come out posthumously (*Economy and Society*, 1922), he points to the solution to break out of the progressive bureaucratic aridity of human affairs and resolve them with a gesture of higher will.

He recognizes that the concept of "charisma" is irrational in nature and unrelated to any traditional norm of behavior attested in society, placed on a revolutionary plane, unrelated to the existing order: "There is the authority of the extraordinary, personal *gift of grace* or charisma, that is, the revelations, heroism, or other leadership qualities of an individual. This is "charismatic" rule of the kind practiced by prophets or—in the political sphere—the elected warlord or the ruler chosen by popular vote, the great demagogue, and the leaders of political parties" (Weber 2004: 34).

It is true that Weber's concept of "charisma" was not intended to justify the establishment of an authoritarian regime, nor was it foreseeable for what purposes such a hypothesis, born out of the need to better value the intellectual freedom of the individual, could be instrumentalized, but one cannot help but recognize that it has been used by totalitarianism in the worst way.

This period is characterized by a continuous alternation of proposals, ranging from the theory of elites by Vilfredo Pareto, Gaetano Mosca, and Robert Michels, to attempts at interpretation from a psychoanalytic perspective by Sigmund Freud, Gustave Le Bon, and Wilhelm Reich, to studies from a sociopolitical perspective by José Ortega y Gasset and Georges Sorel. In all these works, the violent, irrepressible, and elusive character of the masses and the urgent need to remedy them are explicitly highlighted.

Then sociology, from Le Bon to Ortega y Gasset, merely takes note of a new phenomenon and tries to mitigate its negative effects, which are considered deleterious to the social order. At least until José Ortega y Gasset's *The Revolt of the Masses* (1931), he is mainly concerned with the potential force of the masses, studying their violent behavior and, consequently, tracing methods to rein them in.

Faced with such a phenomenon, reactions are diverse, ranging from large-scale oppression to outright rejection of the problem. The two basic positions are distinguished by the possibility of knowing the problem (rational choice) or rejecting it (irrational choice), on which depend as many methods of dealing with it.

True, twentieth-century sociology is largely a conservative science, concerned above all with social stability. Of this tendency to make sociology a useful instrument of social control are first and foremost the classical "élitists," heirs to the Durkhemian conception that wanted society to be led by the upper class. But the great American theorists too, through structural–functionalism and social behaviorism (behavior-mentality); not to be outdone are the rigid interpretations of Soviet Marxism, at the time of "socialist realism."

Interpretations, these, countered by the more open and libertarian approach of Western Marxism, especially thanks to the contribution of the Frankfurt Institute for Social Research (Adorno, Horkheimer, Marcuse, Löwenthal, and Benjamin), the so-called "Frankfurt School," which was forced to move abroad at the time of Hitler's rise to power and, in other respects, the young György Lukács of *History and Class Consciousness* (1923), before its Stalinist turn.

Bauman and the Task of the Sociologist

It would be necessary to wait until the second half of the twentieth century, and in particular, the 1960s, for the attestation of a more radical social critique of the establishment in general and the capitalist system. Since then, sociology has begun to reveal the visionary potential of an atypical science that sets out to imagine the future even before living it, but above all, it reappropriates the "critical spirit," which is the other component, the one left so far in the background, of the sociology of its origins, as it was conceived by its founders.

Subsequent developments move in this direction, up to the denunciation of *The Coming Crisis of Western Sociology* (1970) by Alvin W. Gouldner, which puts an end to any claim to objectivity, in favor of a more decisive subjectification of research. His "reflexive" sociology takes a decisive step toward a greater understanding of human experience and social relations.

Alvin Gouldner, perhaps without being aware of it, marked sociology's entry into the most mature phase of individualism, which was to be established shortly thereafter with Jean-François Lyotard's postmodernity, but he also signaled the need to break out of the impasse of a discipline that was now reattempting to lose its authentic social function.

The prevalence of the "subjective" attitude over the "objective" one entails the strengthening of individualism and its inevitable consequences: the loss of human solidarity, disinterest in public affairs, isolation, and, finally, the breakdown of social ties and traditional community memberships.

Bauman's work, placed at the conclusion of the path taken by sociology over a century, is innovative and, at the same time, confirmatory of the initial intentions of this discipline: excluding any purpose of prediction, it is confirmed not as a tool to direct or condition people, but to imagine and build an alternative future. A science that brings one closer to knowledge of self and the social world. The terms of confrontation are thus reversed, where man and the community are no longer passive subjects, but actors to whom "sociological knowledge" allows free access to conscious choices.

The role of the sociologist, the social thinker, or philosopher of society, is to become a revealer of reality, including those aspects of reality that are not visible or have been concealed. It is for this reason that sociology, in Bauman's lecture, approaches personal issues, lived lives, and individual experiences that, in the totality of events involving everyone, take on social significance.

His words on the fate of sociology are an invitation to revise its status and to bring hope forward, because "Before he may be a thinker, a symbol-maker, a homo faber—man has to be he-who-hopes" (1976b: 101).

Chapter 2

A LIFE IN FRAGMENTS

The secession of the new global elite from its
past engagements with the local *populus*
and the widening gap between the living/lived spaces
of those who seceded and those who have been left
behind is arguably the most seminal of social,
cultural and political departures associated
with the passage from the 'solid'
to the 'liquid' stage of modernity.

Liquid Love, 2003a: 99.

Unlike many sociologists who have preferred to construct an organic and defined system of thought, Zygmunt Bauman is never systematic: he lets himself be carried away by the solicitations of the moment, ready to grasp the signs and tendencies, but always free of any coercion, any self-imposition, any academic obligation. His thought, multiform and complex, can nevertheless be traced back to five fundamental matrices: the holocaust, Marxism, social marginalization, liquidity, and modernity. All unified and, so to speak, held together by a universal glue that represents his most characteristic trait, modernity. Modernity, loved and criticized, excavated and turned inside out, analyzed in depth, is the hallmark of his work, which makes it—together with Max Weber, the other great modern thinker—the necessary complement for understanding our time.

It is no coincidence that this volume starts with Weber and ends with Bauman, marking an intense and tragic century of history, full of dramatic upheavals, accompanied by an unprecedented series of innovations, scientific discoveries, and social and economic changes, which have become the subject of sociological analysis. More so than in the nineteenth century, when it was born from a rib of philosophy, within Auguste Comte's *Course of Positive Philosophy*, sociology was later able to find the right tools to understand social change.

Among those events that marked the twentieth century, the holocaust marked the early part of Bauman's life. Born on November 19, 1925 in Poznań, Poland, to a Jewish family, he fled to the Soviet Union at the time of the Nazi invasion of his country and enlisted in the Polish troops that were part of the Red Army. He fought against the Nazis in Kolberg and Berlin, only to return home (on foot) at the end of the war. In Warsaw, he is one of the youngest majors in the army, receives a cross for valor and studies political science. In those years, he met Janina Lewinson, whom he married in 1948 and by whom he had three daughters (Anna, Irena, and Lydia).

Unlike Zygmunt, Janina experienced the Warsaw ghetto, from which she fortunately managed to escape. Janina's story and the books she wrote on the subject of the Shoa (*Winter in the Morning*, 1986; *A Dream of Belonging*, 1988) prompted Bauman to investigate this issue in depth, whose reflections resulted in *Modernity and the Holocaust* (1989), where Jean-François Lyotard's indications on the close link between rationality and Nazism are confirmed: totalitarian regimes as the most advanced expression of modernity and its deviant need to organize and plan the world, flattening differences and reducing the individual to a mere tool in the hands of the state. An idea that decisively breaks with the common conception of Nazism as an aberration or delirium of incivility and that adheres to the theses of its "normality" expressed by Hannah Arendt in *Eichmann in Jerusalem* (1963).The activity as a professor of sociology at the University of Warsaw and the adhesion to communism are put in crisis by the events of 1956 and the consequent political disappointment, which result in the resignation from the party and in a climate of growing isolation.

As a result of the pro-Soviet government's anti-Semitic campaign, the situation became increasingly unbearable ("We were forced to lock ourselves in the house and not send our daughters to school," Janina declares in an interview), until the painful decision, taken in 1968, to leave Poland and find refuge in Israel. Zygmunt teaches at the University of Tel Aviv, but even here, his intolerance for Zionist politics drives Bauman, in 1972, to move permanently to the United Kingdom, where he accepted the chair of sociology at the University of Leeds.

In England, he begins a new life; he perfects his English and writes directly in this language, immediately gaining international notoriety. He published *Socialism. Active Utopia* (1976a) and *Memories of Class* (1982), where he questions Marxism and distances himself from it. With *Legislators and Interpreters* (1987), in which he analyzed the changing function of the intelligentsia, no longer dominant in a massified society, he prepared himself for the new qualitative leap, tackling the theme of postmodernity.

The new phase coincides with his retirement at the beginning of the 1990s: it is a season of great intellectual activity and well-deserved success, which will make him affirm, on more than one occasion, how preferable it is to leave teaching as soon as possible to devote himself to his studies. After all, he had always greeted academic bureaucratic commitments with ill-concealed annoyance. Having freed himself of those duties, he can finally devote himself to his full-time job in the cottage in Lawnswood Gardens, on the outskirts of Leeds, where he generously hosts friends and colleagues who visit him.

Lawnswood Gardens, a mythical place of intense activity and cultural exchange, will also be the title of the film dedicated to him by Polish director Paweł Kuczyński (2011). The 1990s are the years of the postmodern phase: *Intimations of Postmodernity* (1992b) and *Postmodern Ethics* (1993) mark the transition to a different vision of modernity, which, however, still does not seem convincing to him, leaving out wide margins of ambiguity and incomprehensibility. After *Life in Fragments* (1995), in which he glimpsed a more analytical vision for the social processes of everyday life, marginalization, and the loss of solidarity, Bauman got rid of the idea of postmodernity, considering it inadequate and even outdated, and sought a new model for interpreting reality.

In these years Bauman's thought, while not intending to be systematic, nevertheless elaborated an original theoretical construction, capable of innovating the direction of the social sciences with a decisive methodological turn. Evidence of this are *Thinking Sociologically* (1990a; enlarged edition with T. May, 2001), *Conversation with Zygmunt Bauman* (with K. Tester, 2001b) and finally *What Use is Sociology* (with M. H. Jacobsen and K. Tester, 2013a). Sociology, often reduced to ancillary functions of politics and industry, had in the past limited itself to passively observing society, offering an image of it that was as realistic as it was devoid of any value judgment, according to Max Weber's approach, who wanted it to be a science "ethically neutral." Bauman instead restores an active role in society, empowering it to know and make decisions, making it a conscious protagonist of its future: an approach destined to profoundly modify the subsequent development of the social sciences.

A Sociological Revolution

This second Baumanian revolution—equal, in terms of its impact on the collective consciousness, to the concept of a "liquid society"—modifies the traditional idea of sociology, i.e., of a science that allows one to predict the behavior of individuals and, consequently, also to direct it. Representing in fact, as it has been for a long time, an instrument of social control, albeit without any political purpose: this was the aim of Auguste Comte, from whose positive philosophy, influenced by the growing importance of the sciences in society of his time, sociology was born to study human behavior with the same instruments used by medicine and psychology.

Émile Durkheim, founding father together with Comte, was concerned with establishing the objectivity of social facts by laying down his *Rules of Sociological Method* (1895), but it was above all Max Weber who excluded from the new science any temptation to make value judgments. A noble intention, which has not prevented other social actors from seizing the objective results of sociological research and using them to their own advantage, as a formidable political, economic, or cultural tool.

The depth of his sociological analysis has made Bauman the most representative and listened to *maître à penser* of our time, whose constant critical presence has strengthened and extended since the 1990s, to become the most lucid witness of the crisis of transition between the twentieth and twenty-first centuries. A profound crisis, the roots of which can be traced between the end of ideologies, which characterized the 1970s–1980s, and the economic crisis of 2008.

Other major emergencies converge within this epochal change, including the shift from material to immaterial labor, precarity, and the phenomenon of large-scale migration, with the social consequences that are there for all to see. Added to this is globalization, which began with economic expansion and the acquisition of world markets by large multinationals, and which has proved to be a powerful engine in the process of de-localization of power, capable of demolishing the already fragile system of representative democracy. Without forgetting that the affirmation of new technologies determines the prevalence of immaterial labor, together with the development of communications on a planetary level.

The new millennium is inaugurated by *Liquid Modernity* (2000), which will be followed by a rich series of titles under the banner of the new interpretation of the present, which still refers to modernity, but signals its unstable drift due to the degradation of those symbolic values that had represented its cornerstones until the previous century. The criticism of liquid society does not take on moralistic tones in him but is dense with ethical accents that have humanity, respect for life, and the dignity of existence at their center. The appeal that rises from his pages refers to the radical principle invoked by Emmanuel Lévinas, according to which "everyone is responsible for the other," and invokes mutual solidarity, and equality in the diversity of cultures, opinions, and attitudes. The conviction to remain rooted in modernity makes use of the very idea that liquidity is an inescapable consequence of the process of modernization.

> Forms of modern life—he writes in the new *Preface* to *Liquid Modernity*—
> may differ in quite a few respects—but what unites them all is precisely
> their fragility, temporariness, vulnerability and inclination to constant
> change. To "be modern" means to modernize—compulsively,
> obsessively; not so much just "to be," let alone to keep its identity intact,
> but forever "becoming," avoiding completion, staying underdefined.

[...] After all, it was the quest for the solidity of things and states that most often triggered, kept in motion and guided their liquefaction; liquidity was not an adversary, but an effect of that quest for solidity, having no other parenthood, even when (or if) the parent might deny the legitimacy of the offspring. (Bauman 2012a: VI–VII)

As for the continuation of modernity in liquid times, Bauman's assertion that "modernity is a project of the middle class" contrasts with the current, shared concern about the disappearance of the middle class. The middle class, the one that prepared modernity and defended it against resistance from a decaying aristocracy and a rising proletariat, has been absorbed and then crushed within mass society, where it has lost any identity and privileges.

Bauman is a merciless observer: today's society has changed, it has undergone an almost "biological" mutation within modernity itself; it has taken on a liquid consistency, where points of reference have been lost and certainties are not acquired forever. What seemed established once and for all is continually called into question, destabilized, and withdrawn without warning.

The Other as an Enemy

The consequence of this state of affairs is devastating for society: individualism, loneliness, and mistrust in others prevail, a closure in the private sphere, with the inevitable spillover into the public sphere, politics, and the economy. They induce closure towards the outside; the other becomes a potential enemy and social fears are exacerbated, while commodification, selfishness, and the drying up of human relationships, are increasingly exalted only in social and reduced in presence, and rage.

The social marginalization of the weakest—from the new poor, true "defective consumers," to immigrants, to the oppressed—is the inevitable consequence of a radical change in modernity, which has lost sight of the main purpose for which it was created: the equality of peoples. An equality that, since it could not be guaranteed by birth, could at least be conquered by civilization: equality as the social purpose of modernity, which nevertheless failed to go beyond the process of massification. Liquid society is burdened, in fact, by the decline of the very idea of democracy, as we are used to considering it.

As a result of the process of globalization—that negative part of globalization that nullifies the rights and identity of minorities—power has spread across the planet, it is no longer "localized" in a defined place. The conditions of uncertainty, loneliness, and fear for the future of the global citizen do not find a solution in institutions: thus "society is no longer protected by the state [...] it is now exposed to the rapacity of forces it does not control" (*Liquid Times*, 2007a: 25). The new ruling class is of interclass composition and includes the financial and managerial aristocracy, disengaged from the laws and obligations of nation-states. The new rulers did not need revolutions to assume power, but it was enough for them to wait for the developments of globalization and the crisis of modernity: a process that the bourgeoisie itself triggered, favoring the division between power and politics, but also preventing the realization of equality, which had been the main assumption of its innovative thinking, together with faith in progress.

A Liquid Utopia

After Janina's death (2009), Zygmunt intensified his travels abroad, participating in a whole series of conferences, festivals, meetings, events, lectures, never sparing himself, until his last lectures in Italy, between October and November 2016. In recent years, he has been reunited with Aleksandra Jasińska-Kania (married in 2015), a Polish sociologist whom he had met during his years of teaching at the University of Warsaw.

Despite frequent travels, he does not slow down his publishing activities, even writing three books at the same time. Evidence of his passion is the numerous publications, sometimes written in pairs with other scholars, sometimes the result of conversations, interviews, or even collections of short texts, which followed one another without interruption and were translated all over the world. Of these, the last one, *Retrotopia* (published posthumously in 2017), collects the legacy of Bauman's constant interest in modernity, together with his most extraordinary intellectual creation, utopia, not without pessimistic overtones: if no utopia is feasible in a liquid society, then it is necessary to go back in time, to Hobbes and Spinoza, to a phase when modernity was still at a "nascent state," in a condition of extreme uncertainty, which looks terribly similar to our present.

Recalling the origins of modernity can perhaps help us recover that sense of hope and perspective that has now deprived men of a desirable future. The ability to act rationally, which modernity had promised as a gift and as a guarantee of development and improvement, is undermined at its roots by an erosive flow of instability that takes us back in time, bringing back to the surface existential modes, behaviors, and reflexes of a tribal type, typical of a time when man followed his instincts, driven by the instinct for preservation and the need to satisfy basic needs. The liquidity of which Bauman speaks is not a festive liberating chaos, where everything can be done and undone in the absence of certain rules, but a dangerous step backward for mankind.

With this "retrotopic" message, even in the face of the negative examples of intolerance and violence of which the chronicles are full, his frenetic activity, consumed to the last, in the early days of January 2017, where he continued to write even from bed, comes to a close. He still had much to say, Bauman, especially in the face of the increasingly disturbing signs of a world in which borders are being re-established, barriers are being raised, and nationalistic outlooks that seemed to have been extinguished are being recovered.

What happens to the individual in the liquid society, stressed by uncertainty, isolation, and mistrust, spreads disproportionately to the nation, to the populations, which are also seized by fear of the other, seeing them as an adversary or potential enemy. What was until yesterday observed in the behavior of the individual now becomes a social behavior, a political tendency of many communities/states/governments that fear for their very survival, for their identity, and close in on themselves. In this race backward, in this anxious recovery of the certainties of the past, it is not so much utopias that liquid society needs, as it needs to question the very idea of modernity.

Perhaps, had he had the time, even Bauman would have agreed that that wonderful and authoritative idea of "new time," which had driven the men of the seventeenth century to unite to overcome fear, has now exhausted its historical task. Perhaps, leaving as his last message that unusual idea of "retrotopia," he had begun to reflect on the need to start again from the time before Hobbes, from the eternal struggle between Leviathan, the beast of the sea, and its ancient enemy, the Behemoth, symbol of anomie and anarchy. Perhaps the time has come for Behemoth, the beast of the earth, and we still do not know what awaits us.

Chapter 3

HIGHLIGHTS OF BAUMAN'S THOUGHT

Sociology is different from almost any other area of
intellectual work. Whereas most can identify an object
"out there" which it is their concern to investigate, sociology cannot.
Sociology is itself part and parcel of the social world
it seeks to explore. It is part of a social world
in truth capable of carrying on without the insights of sociology.

What Use is Sociology? 2013a: 9

Zygmunt Bauman was a shrewd observer of modernity and the mind behind the brilliant concept of "liquid society," which is an accurate representation of the current condition of our world, in which insecurity, uncertainty, and individualism are the dominant players.

The depth of his sociological analysis has made him the most representative and heeded *maître à penser* of our time, whose constant critical presence has strengthened and spread since the early nineties, to become the most lucid witness to the crisis of transition between the twentieth and twenty-first centuries. The roots of this deep crisis can be traced back to the end of ideologies that characterized the seventies and eighties, and the economic crisis of 2008. Other major emergencies converge in this epochal change, including the transition from material to immaterial work, the reality of insecurity and the phenomenon of the great migrations, with the social consequences that are visible to everyone.

To this, we must add globalization, which began with the economic expansion and the acquisition of world markets by the large multinationals, and has turned out to be a powerful engine of the process of de-localization of power that can demolish the already fragile system of representative democracy. Moreover, we must not forget that the affirmation of new technologies determines the prevalence of immaterial labor, together with the development of communications at a worldwide level.

Among the major recurring themes that in Bauman's ideas and which have been consolidated in a clear vision of society, we can find the same great insight into the liquidity of the modern world, which involves the breakdown of the relationship between politics and power, considered to be central to the crisis of nation-states, and the evolution of the idea of community, in light of the introduction of new technologies, to which Bauman attributes a large part of the responsibility for the social change taking place.

The Role of the Sociologist

Bauman's thinking, while not being systematic, has nevertheless developed an original theoretical construct that is able to innovate the orientation of the social sciences with a strong methodological breakthrough.

Often reduced to the ancillary functions of politics and industry, in the past sociology was limited to passive observation of society, depicting a picture of it that was as realistic as much as it was devoid of any assessment, according to the perception of Max Weber. Now Bauman restores an active role to society, bestowing on it the gift of awareness and the ability to make decisions, making it the leading player who is conscious of his future— sometimes even with challenging and devastating proposals: if Alain Touraine threw the academic world into turmoil with his irreverent *La Fin des Société* (2013) and its sequel, *Nous, Sujets Humains* (2015), Bauman, in turn, liquidates traditional sociology, innovating it in *What Use is Sociology? Conversations with Michael Hviid Jacobsen and Keith Tester*, 2013a), which was to radically change the approach to social sciences.

This second revolution of Bauman's—which, in terms of the impact on the collective consciousness, is equal to the definition of "liquid society" to mean the current state of instability and uncertainty—changes the traditional idea we have of sociology, i.e. a science that allows us to predict the behavior of individuals and, consequently, also to direct behavior by representing it, as it has been for a long time, as an instrument of social control.

While it did not have a political purpose, this was the intention of Auguste Comte, whose positive philosophy, influenced by the growing importance of science in the society of his time, gave rise to sociology as a means to study human behavior with the same instruments used by medicine and psychology. Emile Durkheim, co-founding father with Comte, was concerned with establishing the objectivity of social facts by implementing his "rules of sociological method," but it was Max Weber who eliminated from the new science any temptation to make value judgments.

This was a noble intention but it did not stop others from taking possession of the objective results of sociological research and using them to their own advantage, as a formidable political, economic or cultural tool. In the end, it was Charles Wright Mills, in *The Sociological Imagination* (1959), who revealed the "visionary" potential of an atypical science that has the ability to visualize the future before experiencing it.

Bauman now, with a *coup de théâtre*, rules out any controlling purpose that sociology could have: it is no longer a science to be used to direct or influence, but to imagine an alternative future. It is a science that allows the acquisition of adequate knowledge and its liberal use. Thus, the very principles of traditional sociology are reversed, whereby man and society are no longer passive subjects, but actors who have open access to choices through sociological knowledge.

Moreover, when asked what solutions there are to recover from the current condition, Bauman never tires of repeating that the sociologist is not a soothsayer or a guru or even an enchanter of the masses. The sociologist is only an observer of social reality. Its universal utility, in very simple terms, is to put mankind in a position to know, to understand, and, therefore, to choose. How the future will turn out depends first and foremost on the people who make decisions on a daily basis on how to act or react to problems. The more clearly they are able to understand the world around them, the better able they will be to understand and learn about the social complexity, with more opportunity to make the right choices.

The role of the social scientist, the thinker, the philosopher or the social critic is precisely to be the "revealer" of reality, even of that part of reality that is not immediately visible or that had been deliberately hidden. For these reasons, the sociology formulated by Bauman closely touches on what is personal, on real life and individual experiences that, as a whole— in consideration of both the small and major events that affect millions of people—take on a social value.

Separation of Politics and Power

The liquid society is also burdened by the decline of the idea of democracy, as we are accustomed to consider it. Thanks to the process of globalization, that is, the negative globalization, which undermines the rights and identity of minorities, power has been spread all over the planet, so it is no longer "localized" in one precise place. The conditions of uncertainty, loneliness, and fear for the future of the global citizen do not find solution in the institutions: thus "society is no longer protected by the state: it is exposed to the rapacity of forces it does not control" (*Liquid Times: Living in an Age of Uncertainty*, 2007a).

The separation of *politics and power* brought about by globalization is another issue that Bauman insists upon. We can no longer fall back on revolutions, since there are no symbols of power to overthrow.

Power has slipped down from its previous level, backing out of the responsibility of citizen control: here is the core of the crisis of democracy: the reference of obligation is in the debate between *democracy and representation*, already discussed by Rousseau in the eighteenth century. We vote for governments and politicians who no longer have the power to act, or to take the appropriate decisions, since power is elsewhere, above the laws of individual states and free to move at will.

"On a negatively globalized planet, all the most fundamental problems— the metaproblems conditioning the tackling of all other problems—are *global*, and being global they admit of no local solution" (Bauman 2007a: 25). The only hope lies in the individual consciousness, in the respect of the self and of others. Equal and different, in a complex society, no longer consisting of standardized masses, nor of isolated individuals, but made up of a network of *multitudes* that are able to talk together and grow.

Extended Communities

Bauman has used the neologism "glocal" to indicate the involvement of the values that belong to the local in a transnational perspective, as if to say: what concrete effects on daily life have the opening of borders and the expansion of the economy at a worldwide level? The first and the most significant consequence of this process is the transformation of the idea of community, which undergoes a sort of "stretching" process of expanding its borders.

What the French would call "le pays"—Bauman explains—is no longer twenty kilometers long, but, say, two hundred kilometers long. You travel by towns, you go to work far away, geographically far away from where you live. So it expands a bit. But also the means of transportation, of connection, with their share of personal experience, expands. There was a development in the past twenty or thirty years; the appearance of digital communication in fact abolished geographical distances, they do not exist any longer, they are not an obstacle. You can travel not only around your community, you can travel around the world without moving from one's own chair. You can sit on your chair and have your laptop in front of you or your i-pad and you can travel and you can have ostensibly, allegedly, seemingly direct experience. I say seemingly because it is not exactly the same as touching each other and sitting next to each other and looking one another into one's eyes. It is not the same, but it looks like direct experience of far-away lands. Very often, connecting with somebody living, let's say, in New Zealand, is easier than to connecting with somebody living next street to you because this one next to you may be busy or not able to talk to you or went on holiday or I don't know what else he might be doing, perhaps he has some personal secret that prevents him from opening the door while you are knocking. But the friend in New Zealand is always there, whenever you push the button he is there. You write to him on Twitter and after a while you have your reply and so on. So it feels like community by it's called "network."

Archaic populations, on the other hand, tried to connect to the land they settled in and gave up nomadism to develop the agricultural economy and defend themselves against their enemies: townships were seen as safe, protected, fortified places.

The concept of community is also archaic. It can immediately be assimilated to hospitality, to a familiar and safe place in which to restore your spirit, where people know you and make you feel at home. In the community you are not afraid, you do not feel alone, but it is a condition that can be stifling and drive you to escape from oppressive control, to cut the strong ties which, though inspired by love and desire for protection, prevent from growing.

But even when you move away, Bauman recalls, the community remains within us as a sort of *imprinting*: the inner core that no globalization will never erase, the last defense of the individual, to resort to in case of need. The co-presence of *communitas and societas* prevails, which the anthropologist Victor Turner referred to back in the sixties, superseding the contrast between *Gemeinschaft und Gesellschaft* that the sociologist Ferdinand Tönnies, and Nietzsche before him, had established as a fundamental cause of the crisis of values of modernity in the late nineteenth century.

These two positions of principle have confronted each other since ancient times and in opposition to them there are those who argue for the protection of their territory, as representative of the traditions and culture and, on the other hand, those who look to the exchange of cultures as an opportunity for growth and development.

If, therefore, a return to the naturalness of social experience, inherent in community, was used to criticize the strong dissatisfaction with modernity and industrialized civilization, today, the essentially authentic part in the "glocal" is destabilized, wiped out. The idea of community has lost its two key features: blood and soil.

This notion of *blood and soil* was important to the German pre-romantics to establish the principles of nationalism. The blood of the strong ties of family and brotherhood; the soil as a privileged territory in which to put down roots. Today they are both obsolete and outdated by the weakening of family relationships (blood) and the opening of national borders (the ground).

Poverty and migration issues are closely linked since the phenomenon of mass migration coming from the poorest countries is directed towards the richer ones, where acceptance and job opportunities can be found. In ancient times this phenomenon gave rise to the process of assimilation. However, now there are no superior cultures in which to integrate and multiculturalism theorizes "the new indifference to difference," recalls Bauman.

It is not enough to talk about the importance of these immigrants without whom the industries and services could not function. The basic problem lies in de-territorialization, that is, in the severance of the privileged relationship with the land in which we live and then calling into question the notion of permanence as a vested right: permanence, this principle of modernity that has been invalidated by open borders.

The evolution of modernity has confirmed the progressive need to erase nationalism. This means that there is no longer a higher law that justifies the occupation of a territory. In globalization, the right to live in an area extends, goes beyond the borders, including the entire planet, and maybe even further still. It is the right to life, to exist, and to enjoy our living space.

The Liquid Vision of Modernity

The metaphor of liquidity is one of the most effective because it is the essence of the world we live in: its *rapidity*, *permeability*, and *mutability*. Stability, and therefore certainty, that characterized the face of modernity in the past, as had originally been established between the sixteenth and seventeenth centuries to ensure economic development through social stability and legal guarantees, is partly being nullified because of that very progress, the evolution of knowledge and technological progress that modernity itself had endorsed. According to Bauman, *liquefaction* is only a matter of accelerated motion and time of observation: the frequency with change happens makes us realize reality as unstable, as well as its consistency and reliability, and will only last for a shorter period of time that does not seem to be long enough. In reality, it is a change of pace, an "optical" phenomenon which also has a considerable impact on our behavior.

The *speed* of events and susceptibility to sudden *change* are combined with *permeability*, because of the development and the ease of communications, which enables information to arrive in real time, reaching every nook and cranny of society, and cause unpredictable effects.

The combination of these elements conjures up an image of a liquid reality that we cannot control, that slips through our fingers and is no longer "manageable." Difficult to keep up with and difficult to predict what direction it will take, until it is already too late, when it has led us to irreversible consequences. Not being able to control has repercussions on us who live in this kind of "interregnum" between a way of life that no longer exists and something stable that does not exist yet—it makes us feel insecure. It is likely that the stability of the future, assuming that there will be a stable condition, will be the effect of an adjustment/formatting of the human mind to the rapidity of change, rather than a slowing down/stabilization of events.

Everything will depend on how we look at it and, therefore, on our ability to observe in a new way, certainly a much faster way, sweeping away those who cannot keep up.

The signs of a sudden acceleration were already present, all of them, and no one could say they were unaware of them. Not only has the human lifespan lengthened and intensified over time, but this change has taken place mainly over the course of the last century.

If we look at the level of knowledge, the ability of contemporary man to know, learn and use his knowledge is incomparably superior to that of his fellowman three to four hundred years ago. It is said, and not without satisfaction, that the amount of knowledge acquired in a lifetime by the average man who lived in the sixteenth century (i.e., the dawn of modernity) would fill the pages of one newspaper today.

In terms of work experience and the social sphere, the increase is even greater: freedom from physical fatigue, more education, more opportunities of leisure and social relationships. During the nineteenth century, the number of working hours per week fell from eighty to sixty; in the twentieth century the working week changed from sixty to forty hours; today in some countries are undergoing a short week of only four days a week.

Even over less than half a century, technology has allowed individuals to travel more quickly from one side of the world to the other, to see and witness events, places and have more information than the human brain can store.

The result of this immense and general advancement of the human condition has its downside: that we are unprepared to receive it without it being a traumatic impact, and cannot prevent being carried away by a great flood which, precisely because of its liquid form, can overcome all resistance and engulf us.

Given that it is a liquid world—*fast*, *permeable*, and *changeable*—the greatest risk we run is to be carried away by the current, oblivious as to what is happening and what our destination is; at the mercy of a natural force that we are not able to control. We can only "react" to the liquefaction of the world, but not "act" independently, and that is what makes humankind uncertain and dissatisfied.

The ability to act rationally that modernity had granted us as a guarantee of growth is now undermined at the very the roots by an erosive stream of instability that takes us back in time; it gives rise to the re-emergence of existential modalities, tribal-like behavior and reflexes, when man followed his instinct, driven by the spirit of self-preservation and the need to satisfy, first and foremost and above others, his basic needs.

To sum up, the liquidity that Bauman speaks is not some kind of festive liberating chaos, where everything can be done and undone in the absence of clear rules, but a dangerous step backward for humanity.

We need to get out of this "interregnum," this enshrouding mire, as soon as possible, and regain our ability to act, to choose rationally and fearlessly the direction we should take, because, as the poet Antonio Machado writes, *"caminante no hay camino, camino se hace al andar,"* and no one can teach us the way forward.

Chapter 4

FROM SOLID TO LIQUID AND BACK

Thus arose the great divide which was to become
the trademark of modern living: one between
reason and emotion, taken to be the substance and the foundation
of all life-and-death choices: like those between order and chaos,
civilized life and the war of all against all.
In particular, the divide separated the regular, predictable
and controllable from the contingent, erratic,
unpredictable and going out of hand.

Alone Again, 1994: 4.

What was Bauman like Before Liquidity?

To get to know Zygmunt Bauman's thought, it is not enough to limit oneself to liquidity, with all its connections and conjugations: it is necessary to go back to his work in the 1990s, when—still involved with the problem of postmodernity—he was sensing the advance of widespread uncertainty (*Alone Again*, 1994) and fragmentation of social relations (*Life in Fragments*, 1995), which followed the better-known *Postmodern Ethics* (1993). During this period of major research commitment, which precedes the turn of the third millennium with the publication of his seminal text, *Liquid Modernity* (2000), Bauman has just left the chair of Sociology at the University of Leeds and can finally devote himself full-time to his studies. From this point on, he publishes no less than sixty volumes and an endless series of speeches, articles, interviews, and lectures, demonstrating how true what he goes on to suggest to his correspondents and friends: leave teaching as soon as possible and devote himself to creative work. Work at the university has become too bureaucratic, and administrative commitments, in addition to exams, leave insufficient time for research, reflection, and writing. 1990 is the year in which he rids himself of this burden, which has become unbearable, not least because of the inevitable disagreements in academia.

He is 65 years old and eager to understand and make understood the society in which he lives. He is studying and writing with alacrity, refining his style, making full use of the English language, which he has mastered perfectly in his long years of teaching, and trying to find a mode of expression that is more comprehensible, closer to the average reader than to his professors' peers. This distancing from the university, which translates into a refusal to use academic, specialized, initiate language, causes him to be looked upon with condescension by his colleagues and even with distrust by other sociologists, precisely because of his choice to stop using the canonical methods of analyzing society. Bauman prefers to talk to people, to make sociology a tool for understanding everyday life, and for this reason the language used can only be ordinary language, that which is most immediate, understandable, and empathetic.

The decade 1990–1999 is occupied by laborious preparatory work: ten volumes, almost a book a year, and the progressive, tireless process of approaching the great insight of liquidity.

The themes are already those of the new social emergencies: inequality and social marginalization, the crumbling of human relationships and the loss of solidarity, and existential loneliness, which becomes the prominent feature of an increasingly individualized society. All wrapped up in the problem of problems, modernity. It is on the discussion, reflection, and rethinking of modernity as a social and cultural construction, as well as a historical and economic one, that Bauman dwells, in an attempt to get out of the closed alley of postmodernity, which he feels is no longer sufficient to define (and thus to understand) current reality.

On the term to be adopted, he discusses at length with other scholars and with a publisher, John Thompson, owner of Polity Press in Cambridge, founded by Anthony Giddens, which has since become his publishing house of reference and will henceforth publish almost all his books. A publishing house founded by sociologists, such as Thompson himself, can only be the ideal host for Bauman.

Postmodernity, a fascinating place that has disrupted the usual ways of looking at the world since the 1970s, on the heels of Jean-François Lyotard's urgings, is too narrow and appears, at a distance, overtaken by events. It was a moment, culminating in the 1980s, of the triumph of the ephemeral, declared the end of ideologies and exalted individualism, but its placing itself on the side of history makes it judged unacceptable. Modernity, Bauman observes, is not over. It has reached a different stage in its development, which is why it wants to be understood properly. It has only changed state: it no longer possesses those certainties, those values that made it a reliable basis for humanity: from solid, it has become liquid.

Very timely are the short texts collected in *Alone Again. Ethics After Certainty* in 1994.

"Being prudent and provident, thinking of the future, becomes ever more difficult, as there is little sense in accumulating skills for which tomorrow there may be no demand, or saving money which tomorrow may lose much of its purchasing power" but above all, "The world, in other words, seems less solid than it used to be (or than we thought it to be)" (1994: 12–13).

Statements written in unsuspected times, which—while preparing for the liquidity turn—are fully consistent with the trends of the time, which Bauman understood well and which were heading in lockstep toward the great crisis of 2008. But the symptoms and forms within which the crisis would manifest itself three decades later (beginning with the pervasive uncertainties that characterize a society ready to burn its assets in the absence of a future) were all already in place, and it would have been easy to take the right countermeasures.

What changed that solid, orderly moment into an unstable, elusive fluid with no landing points?

The causes are many and all are well-known; there are no occult drives, no dark forces that have been plotting behind modernity to erode at the base "all that solid" (to use Marshall Berman's terminology): much of the change has been physiological, thus brought about by the natural evolution of things. Others have been induced by the spontaneous resistance of human beings to act in the face of a threat that does not yet appear to be concrete, whose effects might perhaps have been felt in times judged too far removed from the present and therefore utterly irrelevant.

Yet in the 1990s, when Bauman wrote these texts, the signs were already loud and clear. Jeremy Rifkin was pointing to a coming end of work, André Gorz had pointed to immaterial labor as the future of the world economy, while Francis Fukuyama was even predicting an apocalyptic end of history. Globalization was already a reality and challenged the stability of jobs for millions of people. Behind all this was rapid technological evolution, which was increasingly difficult to keep up with and which was beyond the control of humanity forced to suffer its economic and cultural setbacks.

The computer and the network had already made their overbearing entrance into people's lives; they were no longer just complex working tools for large companies, but were becoming everyday objects for individuals, changing the way people communicated, had fun, learned, and worked.

Behind still was another serious crisis, perhaps less obvious, but no less decisive for the society that was experiencing it with a kind of ill-concealed sufficiency: the crisis of modernity.

Announced in many and varied ways by philosophers (first and foremost by Nietzsche, almost a century earlier), it had come to maturity in the late 1960s.

Cultural upheavals such as 1968 and the French May, feminism and ecological movements, had shown the fragility of a crumbling system, people's dissatisfaction, anger, and irrepressible desire for change. What came to be called postmodernity confirmed the refusal to continue using the "grand narratives" of the past, the great established themes on which the certainties built by modernity over three centuries were based and which preserved the taken-for-granted principles of democracy, freedom, and progress. The ideologies-especially those of the left—which had represented dogmas of unquestionable truth to be adhered to, were suddenly obliterated at the roots; not so much by reason—within which the ideologies themselves had been born-as by an irreverent disengagement greeted with extreme levity: "A laugh will bury you."

To the "deconstruction" of modern solidity, operated by postmodernity, Bauman opposes a consciousness of the self, matured through reason, implicitly following Gilbert Simondon's path of "individuation": what comes to replace ideology, then, is ethics. A new ethic of personal responsibility, guiding the individual through the treacherous path of an existence in which values and certainties have been lost, while landing points—external, solid ones—to which one can sustain oneself have been dispersed. Now these supports must be sought within oneself. The new ethics can only be interior, nurtured by the awareness that everyone needs the other and that, above all, we are all responsible for the other, according to what Emmanuel Lévinas stated.

Only in this way will it be possible to reformulate a politics capable of facing the challenges that await (never was the prediction more just) the society of tomorrow, now deprived of its ancient solidity.

Panta Rhei

Zygmunt Bauman's idea of liquid modernity is based on the perception of a prevailing condition of uncertainty in humanity, to the point of being defined as "the only way there is of the only life available" (1999: 18). It has become such due to the crisis of modernity, which until now had tried to "hold back change" (*panta rhei*: reality as incessant change goes back to Heraclitus), which would have destabilized the social order imposed by centuries of regulations and habits. The certainties we feel the lack are those of modern man, to which he is accustomed, living in a world founded on predictability, and programming, within a grandiose psychological process of "education" to certainties in behavior as in any productive activity. Necessary, certainly, but somehow "forced," since what is natural is, by its very essence, destined to be changeable.

This propensity to change is therefore the very nature of "vitalism," aimed more at promoting life than simply ensuring survival.

When modernity poses the problem of organizing a suitable social form, one that goes beyond the chaotic agglomeration of people on a territory, it is logical that it sought to dictate rules of behavior, set limits, and order, and establish long-term programs that could represent acceptable prospects for life, trying to reduce randomness and uncertainty as much as possible.

Modernity, therefore, is in itself the antidote to social uncertainty. It dictates the rules of existence in the new time according to patterns it considers valid, such as the time of education, work, family, leisure, and retirement. Nothing is left to chance, in a skillful absorption of previous traditional religious practices.

When a "state of crisis" intervenes, one of the first and the most conspicuous effects is the inability to resist the pushes of perpetually impending change for much longer. It is as if modernity, now bereft of strength, is unable to hold back renewal, that inner energy that pushes and overwhelms the dams forged in previous centuries; to dissolve in the air that which had been painstakingly built and which until recently had appeared solid and reliable. It is not just fragility, a weak defense of modern values, but an increasing speed that has turned into an avalanche. As such, it has changed the landscape, rendered it unrecognizable, and retained a friability of the terrain, an insubstantial and soft, slippery mobility, to the point of resembling liquid.

Hence the Bauman metaphor. Individuals driven by disordered movement lose contact with others, they have no time to make up their minds that new impulses take them elsewhere, without even knowing in which direction. This is the full debacle of modernity, which has lost all capacity to hold firm points, leaving the field open to all forms of abuse.

If not liquid, it is still a wasteland where the law does not exist.

Read in this way, it appears to be a tragic and irretrievable condition, so that Bauman's liquid society proves to be a hell with no way out, except in the strenuous defense of the individual, at his own expense and to the detriment of the other. However, it is necessary to take into account the fact that we are still in a state of crisis, that is, faced with a choice, from which it is necessary to emerge in one way or another.

Chapter 5

A PRAISE FOR UTOPIA

"Utopia"
is the name which, courtesy of Sir Thomas More,
has commonly been given to such dreams
since the 16th century; that is, since the time when
the old and apparently timeless routines began
to fall apart, when old habits and conventions
started to show their age and rituals
their seediness, when violence became rife.

Liquid Times. Living in an Age of Uncertainty, 2007a: 95.

Bauman is not just "liquid modernity." The perception that this highly successful media insight is but the last (or perhaps the penultimate) stage of a long and even, at times, contradictory conceptual evolution can be gleaned from his works further back in time, beginning with *Socialism. Active Utopia* and *Memories of class*.

Bauman's lecture is surprisingly "evolutionary," starting from an almost orthodox Marxist conception—see *An Outline of the Marxist Theory of Society* (1964), also belonging to the Polish period, before his move to Israel and then to Leeds—and arriving at a "soft" distance precisely in *Socialism. Active Utopia*, where he privileges the utopian component as an instrument of social growth and liberation, denying value to the ideological and political choices of the Soviet Union.

There are two important references in this book: the praise of utopia as a positive idea and the constant reference to Antonio Gramsci's thought, which Bauman will never abandon, even going so far as to take up the term "interregnum" from the *Prison Notebooks*, using it to define the last fraction of liquid modernity, where previous rules have lost value and new ones have not yet been enacted.

Already in *Socialism. Active Utopia* (1976a), Bauman extolled the utopian principle in its proper, positive sense, warning against the vulgate that wants utopia to be synonymous with unattainable dreams and useless fantasy.

He appropriately recalls that "the blueprints which had materialized were classified as predictions, while the name 'utopia' was kept only for those which failed to do so" (1976a: 10).

Indeed, it would be necessary to return to the original term, used by Thomas More in 1516, and its double, ambiguous meaning of "place that does not exist" (*ou-topia*), but also of "pleasant, perfect place" (*eu-topia*). The little booklet written in Latin would enjoy great fortune, making that intriguing title enter the collective imagination forever: Utopia, the ideal island that does not exist but that one would like to realize at least in a dream: a perfect representation of a society on a human scale, free and happy, administered with measure and respect for all.

"Noplacia" is the place where no one goes, because its perfection is unattainable, but it represents a significant development in the thought of that time: an age of ferment and change that prepares for the Neuzeit, the "new time" that looms, and that a century later another Englishman of the same name, Thomas Hobbes, would reveal through the figure of *Leviathan* (1651), a monstrous representation of the modern state. Attempting to realize the ideal society through an act of submission to the sovereign, which ensures order in exchange for freedom.

"Utopia—Bauman acknowledges—is a thoroughly modern phenomenon" (1976a: 18). Consequently, Thomas More's *Utopia* can be considered a "pre-modern" work, as it conveys an intuition of a time to come that looks to the future, which is not necessarily realized in the present, but rather sacrifices it in favor of a better tomorrow. Modernity, which is preparing to burst into the Western world with its innovative disruptive charge, has a "constructive" and "planning" vision, which makes perfectibility, that is, the concrete possibility of improvement, its key concept. The main tool is given by progress, the idea of perfectibility protracted indefinitely, which represents his unprecedented teleology.

A close link is established between utopia, progress, and modernity, destined to produce long-term effects and change the fate of millions of people. Perhaps this is why, as Bauman suggests, utopia is not a lost dream and an empty hope to be set aside, but something purposeful and achievable for the good of humanity. It is necessary, therefore, to keep in mind that utopia, rather than a futile product of the imagination, far removed from any rational or scientific conception, is instead a powerful engine for building the future: "The presence of a utopia, the ability to think of alternative solutions to the festering problems of the present, may be seen therefore as a necessary condition of historical change" (1976a: 13). And thus, it is not incorrect to say that "utopias do exert enormous influence on the actual course of historical events" (1976a: 16), since they weaken and disrupt habits, lethal to the preservation of the status quo and social subjugation, but above all, they prepare the society of tomorrow, helping to build it in the minds of men and women, before actually realizing it. Utopia, moreover, takes up the legacy of Christianity around the principle of hope and humanizes it, making it a modern quality that drives the realization of a sustainable future.

Hope, a virtue that will also become decisive in Bauman's later works and stand as a principle of salvation and redemption, is the other focal point of utopia. Hope is an integral part of utopia, representing its constituent energy, as well as the very reason for its abiding value for humanity.

For modernity, hope is not just the "last goddess," but a vital principle that allows one to look forward with confidence. Stubborn not to give up, for its death would mean the annihilation of all future prospects, sacrificed on the altar of continuous emergency.

Limiting the future, atrophying it in the withering away of every project, is lethal to the very existence of this virtue, forgotten at the bottom of Pandora's box to alleviate humanity's fear and make it dream. Fear and hope have always been linked: to conquer fear, and endure its consequences, it is permissible to hope. For Seneca, fear follows hope (*Spem metus sequitur*), and Baruch Spinoza, at the dawn of modernity, sees the people coming together under one ruler "more by hope than by fear" (*Majori spe quam metu*).

The construction of modernity takes place by making hope, as well as utopia, the flywheel of society and recovering in a secular key the Christian idea of the hope of salvation. The attribution of a secular meaning to hope, in grasping a cultural issue already attested in consciousness, is among the reasons for the rapid success of bourgeois ethics, grafted onto an already existing "corpus," where the side-by-side with technology tends to replace religious fear with a more concrete, tangible fear for the machine.

The greatest hymn to hope was elevated by Ernst Bloch in *The Principle of Hope* (1954–1959), a colossal work that represents the last chance for modernity to express itself at its best before it begins its inevitable decline.

It is an optimistic work; of that optimism of the will that comes from ideological faith. Bloch, who had greeted the outcomes of the Bolshevik Revolution with perplexity, takes the field with this work of maturity, which is influenced by the "real socialism" proper to the Stalinist period. The hope that flows from this energetic worldview with its totalizing ambition is progressive and hopeful, like Bauman, of the victory of humanitarian socialism. Bloch does not combine fear and hope; fear appears overcome or, rather, removed from consciousness.

Those certainties, so painstakingly reconstructed with the constancy of reason, return to dissipate with the crisis of modernity. There is a risk that hope will give up, allowing fear to triumph; with fear, humanity returns to worrying only about its own survival, cultivating anxiety that pushes to burn everything immediately, without planning, without investing, without waiting. Leaving no room for utopia: that ability to imagine what modernity has taken up, actualizing it, from Plato's *Republic*, fully expresses the essential core of the new way of thinking that is emerging in the Western world. It encompasses within itself the confidence in man's capacity to progress by his own strength—hence the modern idea of "progress," a capacity that hitherto was only in the hands of divinity.

In this process of painful and lacerating separation from a transcendental destiny, aimed at restoring to man the power to decide and choose how to develop his existence, the idea of utopia feeds on a quintessential human quality, imagination. That is, the faculty of producing an abstract thought capable of mentally constructing a fictional reality on the basis of real, experienceable knowledge: it is the faculty of planning, where the mind is able to conceive and "see" in itself something that does not yet exist in reality, but can become so.

But utopia is not just hope, and this is perhaps the most pregnant insight for the historical evolution of this concept in the centuries following Thomas More. Utopia restores the germs of optimism to a humanity hitherto oppressed by suffering: it is happiness and the promise of well-being.

Happiness, in utopian thought, is no longer an abstract concept, but a possible goal worth sacrificing and fighting for, but rather a purpose proper to human existence, a teleology; almost a right.

In this endeavor, socialism completes the framework already expressed by the modern principle of the culture of equality and readily provides the blueprint for a society in which work is not a condemnation, but a satisfying and justly remunerated activity. Let the whole of humanity's efforts be aimed at the progress and welfare of all, so that happiness is achieved here and now, no longer in an otherworldly world.

With this transposition of the "reward" or happiness at hand, modernity successfully completes the operation of detachment from the transcendent and becomes an autonomous force, capable of leading humanity toward a pleasant future, leaving religion to take care of souls, while respecting personal choices as to freedom of faith.

This is almost a "compulsion to happiness," which has been revealed in late modernity as having a counterproductive effect on freedom.

It served, in fact, to justify an operation of social engineering, that is, of manipulation of the individual will to adapt it to the demands of an ordered and homogeneous society, unified in behavior, and forced to follow an externally imposed ideal model. Even by force, when persuasion and conviction were not enough.

Here, Bauman highlights a fundamental aspect of the relationship between the individual and the mass. Fundamental because it explains the radical aversion of leftists to populism. The motivation lies entirely in the necessity of education, that is, the importance of the formation of the citizen within modern society. Education in the broad sense is an adaptation to society, a preparation to fulfill one's duty and assume one's role as a citizen. But also a compulsion to follow the rules of civic and political living within a community regulated by laws and customs. In return, modernity ensures a welfare package that can be spent sparingly throughout existence: these are the well-known "promises" of modernity and include equality, improved living conditions, material progress, and happiness on this earth.

If not everything is achieved by individuals, it will be possible for its children or grandchildren, in a chain of successive postponements that has no end, since it follows the logic of unrealized desire. Alive and effective as long as it remains in its potential state.

But it is only by following the rules and bending to them that it is possible, though not guaranteed, to tend toward the attainment of the promised goals: something that proves difficult at all times, because of the people's low propensity to be educated. Since the eighteenth century, this difficulty was felt and discussed as one of the main problems for the realization of a new society. Jean-Jacques Rousseau discusses this in *Emile* (1762), where the pedagogical tool is shown to be a technology applied to man in order to change him and, consequently, to change society as well. Those who refuse to be educated or are incapable of making themselves autonomous according to reason must be forced against their will by civil or moral obligation.

Out of this arises, almost naturally, a society divided between those who know (the educators) and those who do not yet know (the *educandi*). In this way, rationalism immediately sets itself on an elitist basis that looks at the popular masses with a critical spirit, avoiding pandering to their demands and instead deeming them in need of care, of guidance, precisely, "educational" (from the Latin *ex-ducere*, to bring out).

"D'Alembert—Bauman reminds us, considers the multitude—ignorant and stupefied"; Condillac compares the people to "a ferocious animal," while Diderot finds that "the people are the most foolish and the most wicked of all men" (1976a: 25): perplexing statements from leading exponents of a revolution under the motto "liberté, égalité, fraternité (ou la mort)."

This requires a leadership group to educate and direct the popular masses. Socialism, as the rational project of a perfected society, takes up this need and makes it its own, replacing the ruling group, taking it away from the bourgeois elite, the master class—which would not serve the interests of the people—and entrusting it to the leader of the people, the political commissar, the organic intellectual, the condottiere and then, by a paradoxical chiasm, which subverts the order of things, to the "duce," the tyrant.

All are indiscriminately convinced that they are doing the good of the people, even against their will, because they are lazy by habit, indifference, and apathy.

> It was Blaise Pascal—Bauman notes—who singled out habit and diversion as the two expedients men universally employ to shirk looking their frightening predicament in the face. (1976a: 26)

Fundamental is the question that underlies any conception of freedom: how far it is permissible, ethical, and appropriate to push the coercive force of education (albeit for the sake of good) and how much space of freedom can be granted so that we cannot speak of dictatorship.

The issue is not of secondary importance when one considers that, as "in Stuart Hughes's words, the intellectual leaders began to identify themselves with democracy or socialism, and sought virtue in the cultural pursuits of the common man" (Bauman 1976a: 25).

Bauman accounts for this illiberal aberration and the tragic consequences to which it led, where the socialist ideal of equality was sought to be realized by force, in his early distancing from Soviet communism and in his gradual departure from orthodox Marxism. This book is the real "missing link" in understanding how Bauman's thinking came to a questioning of the concept of class, one of the cornerstones of Marxism, in the later *Memories of Class* (1982). But in 1976, we are still in a phase of reflection, of deep and probably painful conceptual elaboration, which preludes and, in some ways anticipates, the fall of the Berlin Wall.

Morality without Ethics

In several texts in the 1990s, Bauman insists on the ethical problem, both in the three volumes of 1993–1995 and in other scattered essays. In these, he distinguishes between the concept of morality—a "primitive" character, inherent in the human being—and that of ethics, the result of an education, and subsequent learning, which is added to the innate one, though without canceling it.

> Ethics is a concern of philosophers, educators and preachers.—Bauman writes—They make ethical statements—when they speak of the ways people behave towards each other and towards themselves. [...] Philosophers, educators and preachers will insist that to make an ethical

statement it is not enough to say that some people believe something to be right of good or just (1995, 15).

Obviously in postmodernity (or "late modernity," as he defines it, beginning to distance himself from an unwelcome definition), the precepts of ethics are no longer followed: there is no shortage of philosophers, nor educators, nor preachers; the problem is that they have lost their normative force. They have gone *From legislators to interpreters*, as we read in the book with the same title (1987). They are no longer the only ones authorized and empowered to formulate the nomos, the ethical rule, while their place has been usurped by legions of false prophets and even by the common people, in a convulsive pursuit of individualization that arrogates with impunity the right to speak.

And the word of the multitude is the new *nomos*, to be adhered to if it pleases and if it is convenient; certainly not with the question of whether it is right or wrong.

Those who in modernity were both legislators and interpreters, bringing together in one person two absolute powers when it came to deciding on ethical norms, now appear to be deprived of their power in postmodern culture. Deprived of their power as legislators, at most they retain the possibility of acting as interpreters of the affairs of others. Legislators and interpreters (a category in which Bauman probably also includes sociologists, although he does not make this explicit) have no social function other than to stigmatize only *a posteriori* the errors committed and to admonish men and women so that they do not continue to commit them. The spoliation of their aura of sacredness manifests itself in the refusal or impossibility of pointing the way, providing alternatives, and foreseeing the future.

The silence of intellectuals—replaced by the confused and annoying hubbub of their late epigones—is characteristic of liquid modernity, of the last stagnant phase, of that middle age between a world incapable of dictating valid rules (Durkheim's anomie) and a new one that has not yet formed. This middle age, which Bauman first called "interregnum" in 2010, using the effective Gramscian metaphor, is a no man's land, where anyone can stand up and affirm whatever they happen to think and thus impose it, legitimizing it as "truth."

It is the time of multiple and ephemeral relative truths, hence of no truth at all. It is not only a time of uncertainties, characteristic of the previous phase, but of false certainties and post-truths, whose social function is to clear customs of lies and legitimize them as perceived truth, emotionally well-founded and finally "democratic," because they are within everyone's reach.

Bauman of the early 1990s is not sparing in his praise of postmodernity, despite the fact that he sees its destructive tendency prevailing, which "does not seek to substitute one truth for another," but rather proposes itself as "a life without truth, standards and ideals" (*Intimations of Postmodernity*, 1991: IX).

And yet the postmodern condition, which also "seems to condemn everything, propose nothing," so much so that "destruction is the only construction it recognizes," has unsuspected qualities that lie beneath its demolishing eagerness: "the *re-enchantment of the world* that modernity tried hard to *dis-enchant*" (1991: X), along with the subject's capacity to act. The *re-enchantment*, which Weber, at the beginning of the twentieth century, had hailed as a positive component of modernity, together with the recovery of the centrality of the subject, make the postmodern variant appear as a sort of renaissance. And such must have been the impression of those who, including Bauman himself, had seen in Lyotard's notes, around the 1980s, the sign of an expected change. Only to change their minds in the following decade, to the point of abandoning the very concept of "postmodernity" to define that time that had proved so unstable and full of uncertainties. Those same uncertainties that had seemed to herald a liberation from a rigid past, obtusely succumbing to dogmatic ideologies, proved to be dangerously irreplaceable, vacuous, useless, and dangerous. Capable only of disintegrating social ties and future prospects, without creating valid alternatives, denying value to the past, and leaving the individual alone with his present.

> "Liquid-modern" is a society in which the conditions under which its members act change faster than it takes the ways of acting to consolidate into habits and routines (*Liquid Life*, 2005: 1).

Return to Utopia

In his last works, and in particular in *Retrotopia* (2017a), published posthumously, the theme of the unrealized utopia returns with pessimistic veins, in considering how the absence of solidity is causing a poignant nostalgia for the past, where at least utopias fueled the hope of a future on a human scale. "Back to Hobbes," "Back to the tribe," "Back to inequality," "Back to the womb": all symptoms of a retreat to the primitive conditions of life, which nevertheless presaged the birth of modernity and its solid promises. If the time of liquidity is lacerating in its dissolution of the human, it is natural for this disoriented society to turn backward, in an attempt to recover shreds of utopian or "retrotopian" hopes, within a pre-modern condition from which it seems fatal to start again. Bauman looks with sarcasm at this unique opportunity to recover utopia, to go back to the utopias that are more distant, even pre-dating Hobbes, but he is forced to admit the "liquefaction" of modern utopias, and with it of the "promises" of modernity, from equality to dominion over nature; from democracy to the idea of progress. Liquefied utopias that contain germs of hope for a possible improvement, but also the implicit admission that modernity is now a closed issue. An eventuality that Bauman had never before questioned.

Between a despairing liquidity and a longed-for solidity, whose restoration is only a vainly cultivated mirage, Bauman suspends judgment. Not without bitterness. He simply looks up and again urges his readers: "look ahead, for change."

It is no accident that Bauman in *Retrotopia* envisions a recovery of the utopias proper to the period immediately preceding modernity, the only time when utopia, that is, hope for future improvement, could still be effective. That we can go back and restore the nation-state of full modernity is the grand dream that does not displease the right-wingers and populists of the third millennium, nor does it fail to captivate a confused electorate enticed by the mirage of a return to order.

Where order, this time, is not an authoritarian and militarized government, run by the Strong Man, but at least aimed at restoring security, privileging local interests in the spirit of a full recovery of national identity, and traditional and cultural-popular values.

This is the great illusion of the new right, the attempt to go against historical evolution, directed toward the end of the nation-state as it had been realized in the centuries of modernity.

Already Condorcet, in the years of the Enlightenment, had considered the state as a "temporary" institution, destined to run out in time. Subsequent modifications, and adaptations, often achieved as a result of the struggles for democracy, allowed the modern state to establish itself with greater stability and popular consensus, especially through some important innovations, including the separation between its three powers (Montesquieu)—the legislative, executive and judicial—which previously belonged exclusively to the sovereign. Thus in the sixteenth century Jean Bodin had expressed the need to divide temporal power from religious power, an issue that had cost Europe years of religious wars and only ended in 1648 with the Peace of Westphalia, in which the principle of *Cuius regio, eius religio*, that is, of the close relationship between the nation and the religion of the sovereign, was enshrined: if the sovereign was Catholic, the country would be Catholic; if the king was Protestant, consequently the country would embrace Protestantism.

A sanctioning principle that, although it put an end to the Thirty Years' War, would not have been able to withstand the further evolutions of the modern state—the transition from monarchical to republican rule, with its attendant popular sovereignty—unless a process of "neutralization" and separation between *potestas* and *auctoritas* had been implemented. The process of "neutralization" is one of the most significant and decisive for the continuity of the modern state, aimed at making the laws completely independent of any religious and political contamination or influence, but also of any "substantial content of justice and truth," and thus completely "neutral."

The utopia of the latest Bauman is burdened with bitter pessimism in the face of the changes in the negative that characterize today's society. It is no longer the time to advance confidently toward a bright future, but to pick up the threads of the past, patiently rebuilding lost certainties.

One of his *leitmotifs*, "There is a time to fish and a time to mend nets," finds its operational application in his latest work. *Retrotopia* represents an inverted utopia that recovers the past as the *last* resort of rediscovering a hope that modernity has betrayed with incessant repetitiveness. It is the end of utopias, the denial of any expectation of a bright tomorrow, desperately rummaging through the past in search of elements of stability that we can no longer expect in the present, let alone the future.

It is the stagnation of liquid modernity, first seen as an opportunity for change toward an ever-evolving modernity, and thus a modernity not destined to die, but to be reborn in other forms, to deny itself and to re-propose itself. Now reaching a point of crisis that leaves many doubts about its capacity for positive developments.

Ominous signs loom: violence, growing inequality, creeping racism, the rise of reactionary policies, the primacy of populisms, and post-democracy. In order to find signs of a sustainable solidity, Bauman seeks a kind of utopia turned to the past, which has anti-modern, regressive, nostalgic characters. Even reactionary, and even useless. For this passage *à rebours*, he skips feet-first all the time of modernity and looks to the *statu nascenti* of the new time.

Chapter 6

WHEN BAUMAN WAS POSTMODERN

Without resigning its formative questions—
sociology must develop into a *sociology of postmodernity*.
In particular, it must accept the distinctiveness
of the postmodern figuration, instead of
treating it as a diseased or degraded form of modern society.

Intimations of Postmodernity, 1996: 27.

Zygmunt Bauman was one of the most important contemporary sociologists and is universally known for the idea of liquidity, through which he provided a brilliant and convincing interpretation of a rapidly changing reality that has lost the values and reference points of the past.

Liquid modernity, recounted in the 2000 volume of the same name at the dawn of the third millennium, is a condition peculiar to modernity itself, occurring as a result of the social, cultural, economic, and technological changes of the last phase of the twentieth century. By the time he was writing about liquidity, radically revolutionizing the view of today's society, Bauman was well into his seventies, had given up teaching, and retired to Lawnswood Gardens, on the outskirts of Leeds, to write one book after another—sometimes even three books at once—to come out in public only on the occasion of invitations to conferences and lectures, which in recent years had come even feverishly.

Liquid Modernity can thus be described as a work of advanced maturity, a proof of "late style" (*Spätstil*), as Adorno and Said would say, which is affected by the immense intellectual heritage accumulated over time, to which were added the experiences of a long life marked by dramatic events; from the Nazi occupation to joining communism, from World War II to emigration from Poland. A lonely man, co-every exile, never perfectly integrated into the countries in which he lived. Beloved and sometimes misunderstood, judged an outsider in academia because he had little inclination to do quantitative sociological field research. Hated in his own country because of his political background: remembered by Izabela Wagner in her monumental biography: first because of an issue related to anti-Semitism, then because of his pro-Soviet past, which cost him, in 2006, the University of Warsaw's refusal to renew his doctorate (a sort of honoris causa award), held in abeyance pending evaluation of "*previously unknown information*" revealing how Bauman served as "an officer of the communist security authorities in 1945–1953, as well as a secret military information agent, and that he actively participated in eliminating the resistance of the underground guerrilla" (Wagner 2020: 381). Hence the misgivings of some Polish scholars, his former students, and collaborators at the University, and the subsequent regrettable and violent protest that greeted him in Wroclaw on June 22, 2013, when he was invited by far-right groups to give a lecture on Ferdinand Lassalle. Understandable, then, was his decision never to return to Poland.

A Repudiated Conviction

In all his writings after 2000, the year of the publication of *Liquid Modernity*, the turning point of the new century, Bauman rejects the idea of postmodernity: he will never speak of it again and, on the rare occasions when he does mention it, he will deny its historical necessity, gladly quoting Jean-François Lyotard's assertion that "one can't be modern without being postmodern first" (*Liquid Modernity*, 2012: IX).

Bauman himself explains what were the misgivings that led him to renounce the use of the term "postmodernity":

> The so-called "postmodernity" was the time for learning which of the promises of modernity were fraudulent or naive pretentions, which of its ambitions were manifestations of condemnable hubris, and which latent intentions were covered up by loudly declared objectives [...] The term "postmodernity" masked and disguised rather than revealed the true sense of what was happening at the time. The second reason to feel uneasy was the purely negative content suggested by the term. It implied (wrongly, as I tried to point out) what the present realities no longer are, but gave very little—if any—information about their own defining attributes; it called for an inventory of things rejected and left behind, rather than for a reasoned catalogue of things that took their place. (Bauman 2014a: 85)

Yet Bauman, before the liquid turn, was fully and consciously postmodern. Certainly not in a casual way, but a convinced proponent of that innovation so radical for the development of culture, to the point of dedicating to it a number of important studies, including *From Legislators to Interpreters* (1987), *Postmodern Ethics* (1993), *Postmodernity and its Discontents* (1997), and *Intimations of Postmodernity*, published in 1992 by Routledge, whose original title refers to a well-known poem by William Wordsworth, "Intimations of Immortality" (1804). Here the Romantic poet claims the power of recalling childhood memories. But Romantic assonances are not limited here and go instead to looking within postmodernity for signs of a "re-enchantment" of the world, that is, the recovery of that spirituality of which modernity had rid itself in an attempt to make instrumental rationality prevail. In his writings on the *Sociology of Religions*, Max Weber—the leading modern sociologist—had in fact expressed the need to effect a "disenchantment" of the world, avoiding any concession to magic, marvelous, transcendent, yet also emotional thinking that could in any way undermine the goals humanity had set for itself.

A necessary pragmatic requirement, if the world is to be given order, and especially if a stable economic system that guarantees progress is to be built. But it risks losing sight of the human condition when it is resolved in the arid practice of rational relations, as happened in many ways during the twentieth century, marked by the rise of totalitarianism and violent attempts to return to order. In this stance against the risks of excessive rationalism, one can trace the reflections of the earlier analysis on the motivations for the Shoa, which Bauman had analyzed in *Modernity and the Holocaust* (1989), a text fundamental to understanding how in the concentration camps the extreme yearning of modernity to achieve perfection in an orderly and rational world had been resolved—on the basis of Lyotard's own observations.

The Socialist Matrix of Progress

That Bauman has written memorable and clarifying pages on the substance of postmodernism is demonstrated by this volume, which gives a decisive direction to the interpretation of a movement often evaluated with too much superficiality and sufficiency, limiting it to fatuous and spectacular representations, decorativism, pop quotations, and glamorous culture whose purpose is mainly to astonish and beguile.

Instead, from Bauman's words in *Intimations of Postmodernity*, there emerges the need to recover the subject in all its fullness of being, including spirituality and emotionality, along with the desire to return to harmony with nature and the pleasure of happiness.

To do this, postmodernity needed to break with the past, make a clean break with what appeared to be "a long march to prison": to distance itself, with a kind of provocative proclamation of "the end of history." However, voluntarily standing on this side of that three-century period and observing it as a discrete object was not enough. What was needed was a painstaking operation of deconstruction (Heidegger's "Destruktion"), a task that Jacques Derrida's philosophy, among others, provided.

Postmodernity, for Bauman, is also responsible for the fall of communism. His thesis traces in socialism and communism the tendency to achieve rationalized progress, and continuous growth that would overcome the resistance of capitalism, which was instead—by its very nature—inclined to defend immobility and the preservation of achieved prosperity. Clearly, when capitalism itself abandoned heavy industry ("metallurgy," in Bauman's language) in favor of consumerism, the socialist system found itself displaced; it was left alone to defend a rationalized modernity in which no one believed anymore.

As for postmodern threats, viewed from a safe distance of almost half a century, it can be argued that they were mainly part of the climate of uncertainty generated by the loss of values that followed the deconstruction of the past, the end of ideologies, and grand narratives. Rather than having privatized fears, as Bauman writes, postmodernity has exacerbated those same fears, directing them to the plane of existential security and individual loneliness. This is all because the privatization of fears had been a defining characteristic of modernity from its origins. Already in *Leviathan* (1651), the philosopher Thomas Hobbes had pointed to the decision to become a people and gather within the state, under the aegis of a sovereign, as an opportunity to get rid of collective fears. Since then, modernity has set out to erase social fears, but not individual fears. Thus, social fears have been banished and neutralized, in the name of instrumental rationality and its totalizing spirit, and transferred to a more generic and liberating collective responsibility, as the Illuminists and in particular Jean-Jacques Rousseau well understood.

In spite of everything, Bauman was not satisfied with this interpretative key, considered too generic and limited to the deconstructive phase alone, unable to propose anything substitutive. There was a need for new tools of understanding, to begin to understand what "all that is solid melts in the air" could lead to, to quote Marshall Berman, whose work has undoubtedly had a considerable influence on the development of Bauman's thought. Berman writes about declining modernity, taking his cues from Marx, and paving the way for a transformation of modern solidity into something unstable, yielding, and elusive.

From the intuition of those potentials, liquid modernity is born, which in its very expressive simplicity suggests fascinating perspectives.

The postmodern construct is abandoned to its fate as a sterile rebellion to history, like any other tool that has lost its functionality, but it does not invalidate or erase the decisive contribution that Bauman himself has given us to understand its meaning in the most comprehensive way. Indeed, without this passage through postmodernity, it would not be possible at all to understand liquid modernity.

Chapter 7

A MAN IN A WALK

Rather than bidding farewell to modernity,
we are still waiting to gather the fruits
of its promises and keep consoling ourselves that,
this time over, they are really round the next corner
or the one after that. The promised fruits are comfort,
convenience, safety, freedom from pain and suffering.

State of Crisis, 2014a: 74–75

"A man in a walk" is not a metaphor. Zygmunt Bauman liked to walk at a good pace. He often did so in the morning in the woods behind his house in Lawnswood Gardens, a residential suburb of Leeds.

One day, he told me that at the end of World War II, in which he had participated by serving in Berling's Army, the Polish section of the Soviet Army, he had walked home from Berlin to Warsaw.

Such was the desire to leave behind the hell of war and return to normalcy. All his life, he continued to give the idea of a man on the road. Advancing without hesitation, without compromise, without shortcuts. Above all, without the help of others, but "together" with others. And without climbing on the shoulders of giants, because giant he was himself.

The proof of having encountered a great personality who took giant steps without shirking contradictions, afterthoughts, and the tópos of consistency is found in the divergence between the Bauman before the liquidity turn and the one after.

The Bauman we know is inextricably linked to the idea of liquid modernity, but it is no less interesting and useful to know "Bauman before Bauman" (in *The Bauman Reader*, 2001), when the Polish sociologist, later transplanted to Leeds, comes into contact with postmodernity, senses its innovative potential, its intellectual stimuli, espousing its concepts.

This book, edited by one of his earliest scholars and friend, Peter Beilharz, a professor at La Trobe University in Melbourne, Australia, is a useful collection of the most significant texts, just from the period before the introduction of the concept of liquidity, having been compiled in 2000, while Bauman was giving *Liquid Modernity* in print.

First enthusiastically espoused, postmodernity was then abandoned in favor of liquid modernity at the turning point of 2000. Since then viewed negatively precisely as a function of that "post," which indicates something that comes later, that is finished, while Bauman then matures the belief that modernity is not finished at all, but has changed its face. The postmodern is thus abandoned, permanently erased from his vocabulary, like an infected refuse to be quickly rid of. It remains a temporary episode, a critical phase of modernity, an illusion of individual self-consciousness that is now outdated.

Anti-Academic Par Excellence

Bauman has played the role of "wandering Jew" in the practice and complexity of his thought. Raised little by little, amidst a thousand difficulties, obstacles, misunderstandings, and disappointments. An outcast in his homeland, Poland; removed from teaching because of anti-Semitism, forced to repair to Israel. From there, again uncomfortable with Zionist politics, a new move to Britain, a new language with which to communicate, write, and think.

Leeds, where he taught from 1971 to 1990 and lived until his death, was the last refuge of an exiled life. Always as a guest, never as a host.

Leeds, not Oxford or Cambridge. Leeds, not Harvard or Yale in the United States. A defiladed university location, indicative of a twofold significance: academia's lack of attention to him and Bauman's impatience with academia, demonstrated by his decision to leave teaching early to devote himself to his studies. Suggestion that he gladly bestowed on friends and that had infected his most beloved student, Keith Tester, who died prematurely in January 2019 after leaving the University of Hull, where he had been called to the chair of sociology.

Academia has never been soft on Bauman. Judged with condescension, as one does with an outsider, an uncomfortable visitor; accused of not having done field research, those big analytical projects that comport the involvement of several people, the allocation of adequate funds, long time frames, and results that are incontrovertible because they are based on statistical data. But how could anyone think that a personality like Bauman, an anti-hero par excellence, would set out to lead such undertakings?

Such operations are suitable for incardinated, stable professors, perfectly integrated in an environment tailored to them, surrounded by assistants, researchers, technicians, and collaborators. Bauman didn't even have a secretary to keep his complex mass of materials, texts, notes, and correspondence in order, so he often happened to deliver the same text to different recipients or insert the same passage twice in two separate essays, believing he had not yet used it. A "Collateral damage" caused by imperfect computer use and haste.

Looking at Bauman's extensive bibliography, the "distance" between his pre-1990 production, when he was still teaching at Leeds, and his later production, after he left teaching, immediately jumps to the eye. Which seems to give reason for his decision to leave the scholastic commitment as soon as possible. But not only that: international success, and unanimous recognition, even from academia, came only in the latter part of his life. Significantly after the 1990s, it exploded uncontainably in the early years of the third millennium, coinciding with the liquidity turn.

Again staying away from the universities; among the people, in the squares, at festivals, beginning at the Modena Festival of Philosophy, of which he had become a regular guest since the first edition in 2001.

The Holocaust as a Product of Modernity

The centrality of the pre-liquidity period is given by the theme of the Holocaust, which brings about a radical shift in the evaluation of modernity itself in an unexpected and radically innovative sense, compared to the traditional historical interpretations that had hitherto followed one another, from Hannah Arendt to William L. Shirer to George L. Mosse. Bauman had not had the opportunity to reflect on it in depth, and probably never would have done so, had he not received the stimulus to reconsider that tragic event from reading the book by his wife Janina who, unlike him, had experienced the Warsaw ghetto firsthand and retained the shocking memory.

The decision to write the diary in two volumes, *Winter in the Morning* (1986) and *A Dream of Belonging* (1988), at the urging of Bauman himself, was then decisive in maturing some original considerations on the inherently "modern" nature of the Nazi project of domination over man: science as eugenics, the technique of the crematoria and the war machine, the centrality of the state, totalitarianism as the annihilation of individuality to build a homogeneous and subordinate mass, to be used indifferently as labor power or meat for slaughter.

If the Holocaust is not strictly related to Germany, but a less generically "modern" phenomenon, it should more precisely refer to all totalitarianism as an attempt to rationalize the world and control the population of a state.

It is Bauman's great insight, expressed in *Modernity and the Holocaust* (1989), that changes since then the judgment on modernity, prepares the ground for a tighter analysis of the loss of social solidity, and accompanies, complementing it, Emmanuel Lévinas' statement on Nazism as an extreme and perverse refinement of modern rationalism.

> The Holocaust was a characteristically modern phenomenon—he writes—
> that cannot be understood out of the context of the cultural tendencies and
> technical achievements of modernity. (Bauman 1989: XIII)

The argument is more generalized and disturbing: then it is modernity itself,
in its intent to make the state the unifying entity of individual individualities,
that leads toward totalitarian drift. A drift that would represent the ultimate
goal of a process that depresses the subject and his freedom, making technology
the main instrument of domination over man and nature.

Now the vision is clear and the historical process that has brought
contemporary man to the condition of uncertainty and insecurity is well
outlined in its development. It is now possible to look around with greater
clarity and critical spirit. To move forward.

The Re-enchantment of the World

Sociology, on closer inspection, is also a product of modernity, of its original
purpose to "control" the world, identifying its laws of behavior, and its
tools for preserving social order. And it is significant that subsequent to
postmodernity—from the 1970s onward—after a laborious process of
re-enchantment of the world—where, as Max Weber recalled, modernity
had provided for a necessary disenchantment of the world—critical sociology
developed that reversed its instrumental stance in favor of constituted power
and turned against it. Making itself the subject of human liberation and
understanding of political and social conditions.

A process that departs from the Frankfurt School, through Charles Wright
Mills, Herbert Marcuse, and the '68, and arrives at the reflexive sociology
of Alvin W. Gouldner. Bauman is the point of arrival, the moment when
sociology's long march of enfranchisement from the constraints of modernity
comes to full consciousness, ready to move beyond the conceptual limits of
postmodernism while preserving its innovative lines.

The crisis of modernity is not only the end of solid certainties but also the
possibility of restoring to humanity the "re-enchantment of the world" that
had been taken away from it along with full individual autonomy.

Re-enchantment here does not mean the abandonment of the processes
of intellectualization, rationalization, and technicalization that distinguished
the transition from feudalism to modernity, but rather the detachment that
postmodernity assumes vis-à-vis reason, recovering the value of the emotions
and aesthetic pleasure, along with the perplexity toward a technique that
is too invasive and harmful to nature, the distrust of science removed from
human control.

The re-enchantment of the world is then a recovery of the "naturalness" of the human condition, as demonstrated by ecological movements and the importance assumed by the individual in contemporary society, the prevalence of the subject, and its existential and emotional frailties.

That condition which, for all, has now been identified as proper to liquid society. It is from here that Bauman resumes his tireless journey with renewed energy and great hope for the future of humanity.

Last Comes the Interregnum

Perhaps tired of seeing his idea of "liquidity" trivialized, in the second decade of this century, he introduced the concept of "interregnum," borrowing it from one of the thinkers through whom he had matured his Marxist beliefs since his youth: Antonio Gramsci.

What Does it Mean to Live in the Interregnum?

The interregnum is not just a time between the end of one reign and the beginning of another. It is also a place of transit, a post station where one stops and waits for the next bus (or train, or plane) before continuing the journey. Its presence is not occasional, but planned well in advance and organized in every detail so that the change is as comfortable and short as possible.

The speed of each transition is essential, as lingering in the exchange zones can be dangerous. One can have bad encounters, one can get lost; in each free zone separating two territories—the known place from which we come and the next destination—unusual rules apply, the usual guarantees are suspended, personal identity is momentarily replaced by the temporary identity of an anxious passenger, whose only concern is to get out of that precarious place unharmed and resume the journey in a safe vehicle.

One understands how the interregnum passenger is an even more fragile man, unsure of himself, uncertain of what to do, focused on his own person, and oblivious of others. This is the reason why every interregnum period is carefully accompanied by special safeguards, which set its duration in very narrow terms: a predictable and as painless as possible transition.

There are, however, unforeseen transitions, if not left to chance by those whose task it was to take care of them and organize their advent with due care. These are the most disastrous transitions, the ones that—as Gramsci understood—weigh most heavily on human beings and produce morbid effects. The unpredictability and unpreparedness in facing the change leaves one shocked, especially because in the confusion of the moment one does not know which means of transport (bus, train, or plane) one will have to board, nor what the next destination will be. The interregnum, instead of being a comfortable and brief place to rest, proves to be an oppressive and depressing hell from which one does not know how and when to get out.

One is forced to face an unwanted existential condition, where one suffers, moreover, the three consequences indicated by Bauman that characterize the unexpected: ignorance, impotence, and humiliation.

The first, ignorance, because we have lost the coordinates of the territory in which we live; we do not know where to go, nor what behavior to adopt in the face of the novelties encountered, the emergencies we face; not even our previous experience can help us, since in the interregnum, it has lost its validity. We are confused, we need to learn new things, but there is no one to teach us.

The second, powerlessness, is terrifying because it prevents us from acting: we remain immobilized in the knowledge that we can do nothing to get out of it. The only hope lies in waiting, consumed in the futility of everyday life and the fulfillment of biological obligations necessary for mere survival. Still and incapable of any change, deluded that frantic communication with others, the exchange of information, and the multiplication of virtual relationships can overcome loneliness and represent a form of action.

The third, humiliation, is the corollary of the previous ones; it makes one lose self-confidence, and become dissatisfied and aggressive. Aggression, which culture, education, and civilization have put to sleep, re-proposes the instinctuality of human reactions in a decomposed form. It takes us back to antiquity, to the pre-modern, to the *homo homini lupus* relationship that Hobbes intended to remove with the force of the Leviathan, the monstrous formation of the state composed of all men gathered in the solidarity of the people. But today, the Leviathan is dismembered, it no longer has the strength either to unite or even to defend: everyone is left to his own devices, in a swamp where social bonds are for the moment suspended or at least "under construction," so that every other human being is a probable competitor or even an enemy to beware of.

Unde Malum

What are the origins of evil? Man has never stopped asking this question, always finding new explanations that do not prove to be exhaustive. To answer this question, it is necessary to complete Augustine and Severinus Boethius' phrase, "Si Deus est, unde malum?" If the world was created by God, where does evil come from? Here lies the error, since from such an assumption can only derive an interpretation of evil as an exception, as an accident of the road. Something foreign to our world, but which, precisely because of its occasionality, can be delimited and combated. Because it is difficult to accept the idea of evil as an inseparable part of human nature, the Enlightenment tried to defeat it with reason, but every attempt proved counterproductive because evil feeds on rationality and the idea that it lurks in ignorance and the darkness of superstition seems erroneous. Evil can take advantage of modernity, born of progress and technology. As Lyotard wrote, the culmination of modernity coincided with the holocaust, the most tragic but perfected example of a rational institution with an alienating destructive lucidity.

Reason has failed, although a recent study, *The Better Angels of Our Nature* (2012) by Steven Pinker, shows how genocides and conflicts have decreased over time. A comforting fact, which however does not explain the massacre, as psychologist Sternberg notes, of over one hundred million civilians, almost an average of three thousand per day for each of the 36,525 days of the twentieth century, despite the civilization process.

The question is still: "Unde malum?" Fifty years after the publication of Hannah Arendt's *Eichmann in Jerusalem* (1963), written on the occasion of the trial of Adolf Eichmann in Jerusalem, one is still surprised by the disturbing "normality" of the Nazi executioners. Ordinary people, dutiful government officials, and petty clerks who were guilty of the most horrendous crimes against humanity carried out what they believed to be their duty. To consider the holocaust, a unique and unrepeatable phenomenon is to look away from reality. In *Collateral Damages* (2011a), Zygmunt Bauman goes further and investigates the seemingly incomprehensible gap between the behavior of a "decent" person and the subsequent perpetration of a wicked deed, revealing new traces in Günther Anders' Prometheus complex, in man's sense of inferiority before the destructive power of the machine. But evil today appears more and more like an "economic necessity," on a par with the bombs dropped on Würzburg (Germany) at the end of World War II so that they "would not go to waste."

Evil as brought about by development or growth is almost a "collateral damage" of progress because it is a consequence of production, of the struggle for hoarding, of the maintenance of differences, and, ultimately, of man's cynicism and impotence.

Chapter 8

DEVOURING DEMOCRACY

> Margaret Thatcher's infamous catchphrase
> "There is no such thing as society" was simultaneously
> a shrewd reflection on the changing nature of capitalism,
> a declaration of intent and a self-fulfilling prophecy: in its wake,
> there followed the dismantling of normative and protective networks,
> which greatly helped the word on its road to turning into flesh.
>
> *Liquid Modernity*, 2000: 64.

The uroboros is a snake biting its own tail, an alchemical symbol of power that consumes and regenerates itself. But of the infinitely repeating circularity of time too (Friedrich Nietzsche). For Nancy Fraser, a radical philosopher at the New School for Social Research in New York, the uroboros may well represent capitalism. In *Cannibal Capitalism: How Our System is Devouring Democracy, Care, and the Planet—and What We Can Do About It* (2022), she hypothesizes its ability to grow disproportionately through the self-propagating practice of the very elements that serve its survival. It cannibalizes the riches of nature, above all, without providing for their reintegration, along with care work, whose energies are diverted elsewhere, and even political capacities, deprived of all decision-making power, with a continuous work of exploitation and expropriation at the expense of the weakest people. Despite this continuous self-destructive activity, capitalism manages to progress and regenerate itself, in defiance of all logic. Fraser has no doubts: starting from a thesis that seemed outdated, he translates it into a manifesto of social and economic criticism with very harsh tones. In fact, capitalism was hardly spoken of anymore, it seemed an obsolete, "ironworkers" term, out of place in times of immaterial labor, financialization, and globalization. Even the classic equation capitalism = class struggle seemed to fall by the wayside. What is the point of class struggle without capitalism? The last time was in the pages of Marshall Berman (*All That is Solid Melts into Air*, 1982), but it was in the 1980s. Starting from a statement by Marx, Berman wrote that capitalism is by its very nature mutable, precisely because it is modern. It is unstable, it feeds on continuous modernization, and it consumes resources, ideas, products, and fashions. It creates new balances, following an incessant process of dissolution and recreation. If you want to counter it, you have to ride the change and perhaps precede it. Much remains of Berman's idea, perhaps through Bauman and his idea of liquidity, in Nancy Fraser, thanks to whom we discover that capitalism had fueled the various crises that followed, including the pandemic, only to return stronger than ever each time. What perished were, if anything, its opponents, duly cannibalized or co-opted into its service.

Because there is one point on which she insists: that capitalism is not an economic system, but a social system. Born with modernity, it made the first major break with the past by separating "waged productive labour" from "unwaged reproductive labour," with a clear division of roles. (Paid) production was reserved mainly for the male gender and (unpaid) reproductive and care tasks for the female gender, thus determining "modern capitalist forms of women's subordination." Together with systematic exploitation and expropriation of wealth, to the point of disenfranchising the very productive and reproductive agents from which it draws its support.

It is in this irreconcilable contradiction, in this continual dispersal and cannibalization of the natural, human, and political riches that support it, that capitalism grows stronger. Fraser's analysis is radical, wide-ranging, almost global in its understanding of events and trends, offering the reader a lucidly destabilizing overall view of the idea we have of a society that tends to be progressive, which still has to come to terms with so many critical issues and inequalities.

Fraser warns that in order to understand the real status of our world, it is necessary to go digging into the "hidden seats" of production. One will find that capitalism as a way of life, firmly entrenched in the minds of modern humanity, in its protean capacity, has taken on reassuring faces and manifested seemingly innovative solutions, on which collective criticism has poured in. As in the case of neo-liberalism, which is none other than the old capitalism in disguise, useful for diverting general attention toward secondary objectives.

In the end, Nancy Fraser does not come up with any solutions, except that of "starving the beast." Not an easy goal, if after centuries of struggle and hard-won (partly withdrawn) achievements, we still depend on Marx's ideas on Capital. Today's increasingly individualized society seems to have solved general problems on a strictly personal level, but always within the same logic of value accumulation. The privatization of lives reserves to each individual the task of solving his or her own problems, without affecting the system as a whole. It is a form of survival based on a tacit agreement between the individual and the big cannibal: the important thing is to leave the small personal space in which to act intact. While waiting for the right solution, which will not come about by starving the beast or even through a revolution, it is better to rely on the hope of a slow decline. If capitalism was born with modernity, only the end of modernity would be able to erase the "hidden seat" in which the culture of capitalism was born.

It is only a matter of time.

Chapter 9

THE MULTIPLE DECLINES
OF THE WEST

The road to future turns looks uncannily
as a trial of corruption and degeneration.
Perhaps the road back, to the past, won't miss
the chance of turning into a trail
of cleansing from the damages committed
by futures, whenever they turned into a present?

Retrotopia, 2017a: 6

Is there a decline of the West? The impression shared by many that we are going through a period of crisis of the values and fundamental principles on which our culture has long been based, has distant roots, which the most serious economic crisis of 2008 has only amplified and made tangible in the lives of millions of people. It started with the end of the "great narratives" and the collapse of ideologies that Jean-François Lyotard (1979) spoke of in relation to post-modernism. It was the 1970s and it was yet to manifest itself in the more drastic "liquefaction" of society indicated by Zygmunt Bauman, who admirably described the dissolution of a consolidated system, identifiable with modernity, and which involved economic relations, social relations, and the very legitimacy of the nation-states born from the Peace of Westphalia onward.

It is the latest "decline," the one that concerns us directly, but which follows several moments of crisis that are dispersed in the distant past. Beginning with the controversial vision of Oswald Spengler, the author of *The Decline of the West* (1918): a "cursed" book, to which we owe the pessimistic definition of a world in ruins that awaits a vitalistic and, perhaps, authoritarian rebirth.

Branded as an irrationalist and forerunner of Nazism by György Lukács in *The Destruction of Reason* (1954), Spengler did no more than pick up on the malaise of a time of confused ambitions and uncertain relations with technology, where war seemed the adequate solution to every problem.

It had such a powerful and lasting effect—writes Lukács—because Spengler gave this change its most radical expression. It was the representative work of this phase and at the same time a veritable, direct prelude to fascist philosophy. (Lukács 1980: 461)

War is seen for the first time as the real opportunity for redemption, growth, and change (war as the "only hygiene of the world," according to the Futurists). The expected opportunity to suddenly change the humiliating condition of moral decay and political immobility that was forcing Europe into spiritual decadence. In this exalting (and exalted) vision of war as growth (Max Scheler, 1915), which even Max Weber did not shy away from, in the conviction that Germany had a leading role to assert, the Darwinist theory of evolution in its racist variant, "social Darwinism," is not alien.

And finally, adding to the approval for a liberating war, as the right practice to solve the problems of society at the time, was the belief—later proven wrong—that the new wars would be fought by machines.

A man-driven machine war, but without the cost of human lives, fought far from urban centers, in the air, or at sea, thanks to the use of those new contraptions that were submarines and aeroplanes, was the best that could be wished for to change the world.

In this bitter disappointment, in this evident demonstration of the disastrous effects of World War I—a climate in which Spengler writes—the ideological presuppositions, steeped in revanchism, are already present, which in Italy will lead to fascism, through the myth of the mutilated victory, and in Germany to Nazism, through the delirium of *über alles* domination and the purification of the race.

The machine with its human retinue, the real queen of this century, is in danger of succumbing to a stronger power. But with this, money, too, is at the end of its success, and the last conflict is at hand in which the Civilization receives its conclusive form—the conflict *between* money and blood. The coming of Caesarism breaks the dictature of money and its political weapon democracy. [...] For us, however, whom a Destiny has placed in this Culture and at this moment of *its* development—the moment when money is celebrating its last victories, and the Caesarism that is to succeed approaches with quiet, firm step—our direction, willed and obligatory at once, *is* set for us within narrow limits, and on any other terms life *is* not worth the living. We have not the freedom to reach to this or to that, but the freedom to do the necessary or to do nothing. (Spengler 1926: 506–507)

Spengler's assumption is not a new one; in addition to Nietzsche's critical position on modernity, it takes up Ferdinand Tönnies' opposition between *Kultur* and *Zivilisation*, and combines it with the idea of the cyclical nature of historical events already suggested by Greek Stoicism and then, in the eighteenth century, formulated more decisively by Giambattista Vico with the theory of courses and recourses.

According to Spengler, civilizations have moments of development, full affirmation, and then inevitable decline, corresponding to the cyclical succession of the seasons. Spengler rejects causality and privileges analogy: starting from the observation of historical facts, he intends to create a universal science where, in deference to Ranke, "every epoch is equally close to God"; an affirmation that marks the cancellation of the idea of progress in history and its replacement by a series of "events" unrelated to each other, which fall outside a cause-effect sequence: a concept proper to Edmund Husserl's phenomenology (1913), later taken up by Martin Heidegger in *Being and Time* (1927).

His invective against the power of money denounces a lack of competence in economic processes, almost at the level of "a helpless dilettante," as Theodor W. Adorno writes, for whom he "speaks of the omnipotence of money in the same tone that a petty-bourgeois agitator would use to rant about the international conspiracy on the stock market" (Adorno 1997: 67).

The same concept of "socialism" proclaimed by Hitler seems to come from Spengler, and in particular from his writing *Prussianism and Socialism* (1919), where he considers that true socialism—present in many phases of history, from Stoicism to Buddhism—is already present in the Prussia of Frederick William I, as a "suprapersonal community," as opposed to the individualism and independence of the individual, characteristic of countries like Great Britain. There is in this vision a blatant contempt for democracy, which will burden all right-wing ideologies and will be used by fascisms to exalt the pliability of the mass, which in Spengler is still in the form of the "Fellah," hence the crowd, unknowable, occasional, fickle, and passively guided by the superior will of the "Caesar" on duty.

But the decline lurked deeper, already within modernity itself, whose parable—in the words of Friedrich Nietzsche—was inexorably coming to an end. An end too many times announced and always postponed until a later date, like a "long goodbye" from a beloved place from which one does not want to leave, combined with a feeling of regret and historical necessity, just like Walter Benjamin's *Illuminations* (1969) who leaves a ruined world looking backward.

If the first signs of an inevitable decline were perceived by reactionary thought, to which Spengler rightly belongs, with the inevitable conclusions that are not exactly agreeable, today, when the great promises of modernity—democracy, freedom, equality, and progress—are called into question, the threat of a decline of the West takes on a very different meaning from that expressed by Spengler and his epigones. If it is true that it is not possible to compare the historical period in which Oswald Spengler wrote his Sunset with today's reality—being too distant and incompatible with the conditions of the world of a century ago—it is, however, impressive to see the recurrence of crisis situations so frequent. The West is in perennial decline, announced several times with unaltered alarmism, always on the verge of losing its hegemony, its effectiveness, and its centrality in the world context. It is a bumpy ride from Spengler's tragic predictions—drawn up in the years immediately preceding the outbreak of World War I and published immediately after the end of the conflict—in the wake of that Nietzschean pessimism that proposed a return to man's naturalness against the disastrous effects of industrialization, to the evident signs of the primacy of the East. China, in the first place, is the new hegemonic power preparing to condition our near future.

The last century has been an uninterrupted succession of symptoms of decadence, both economic, political, and cultural. The same social liquefaction denounced by Zygmunt Bauman (2000) merely serves as a sort of "limited sovereignty": it is effective and justified only in this part of the world, Europe and North America, which the other inhabitants of the planet, non-Western and non-Westernized, look at with trepidation as one looks at a protected species threatened with extinction.

From our point of view, from our observatory—for the moment still privileged—we continue to consider the rest of the world with the conviction that we are at the center of it. A sense of superiority that we cannot shake. Even when traveling from one continent to another, physically or through real-time images, we continue to perceive convincing signs of a supposed Western hegemony. Whether it be Coca-Cola or rock music, fast-food or sport, we do not even realize that those elements/leftovers/leftovers of culture that we exported, with the intention of globalizing and colonizing others with our taste, imposing habits, fashions, behaviors, vices and (few) virtues, thinking we could impose the primacy of civilization, have been largely metabolized, digested, transformed, and adapted to local needs: all that remains are the outward signs, dazzling neon lights that attract the eye, but do not go beyond an exotic trait, an aesthetic value. These are ephemeral, apparent victories. The temporary victory of the West has long been undermined by the broader crisis of modernity. Because modernity and the West have close ties, living in symbiosis with each other. The modernity we know, among the many possible modernities, according to Shmuel Eisenstadt's stimulating thesis (2006, pp. 3–34), is uniquely the West's; it is its intrinsic characteristic, one dragging the other downhill in a downhill race that cannot be stopped, only slowed down. It is true that the moment in which Spengler wrote has nothing to do, historically, with us, but what unites yesterday with today, the direct thread linking the existential malaise and unease of the early twentieth century with the crisis of the third millennium is still called "modernity." Clear symptoms of decline lurk deep at the very roots of modernity, whose development seems destined to come to an end after the parenthesis of postmodernity and liquid modernity. It is, on closer inspection, an end that is announced, invoked, perhaps feared or underestimated, always postponed sine die; the conclusion of an era and an existential mode that has become familiar and, for this reason, difficult to give up. Today as yesterday, the underlying reasons are the same and are well rooted in the drift that painfully accompanies us out of a historical condition that has had its day. What remains of Spengler and his idea of civilization destined to perish cyclically is strongly conditioned by the tragic events that he perhaps unintentionally (or perhaps not) helped to bring about.

But how many declines of the West have followed one another? Since Nietzsche, the decline of the West has been announced countless times. In the years between the two world wars, an impressive series of "prophets of doom" concentrated on denouncing the evils of modernity, the disappearance of values, and the dissolution of the individual in mass society. From what we read in the various declinations given by observers, the main issue seems to lie in Europe's loss of hegemony. A hegemony that it had self-assigned to itself when building what has been called "modernity." The decline, at first imperceptible, then increasingly rapid, accentuated by the events of the last decade, has made it clear that Europe did not have a monopoly on modernity, but that the multiple modernities that developed differently—and which did not necessarily coincide with a state—had their own ways of understanding and declining it. Between the eighteenth century and the present, multiple modernities have grown and taken on different faces, only to end up clashing with each other at the moment when globalization, that is, real-time communications and the fall of borders—first economic and cultural, and then physical—has allowed free exchange not only between cultures but also between the identities of peoples and places.

The realization that there are no superior cultures that can arrogate to themselves the right to impose on others, by good means (the idea of development) or by bad (colonialism), their own model into which to integrate, has undermined Europe's centrality in the world, hitherto shared with the other great western power, the United States of America. Already by the end of World War I, the years in which Spengler writes, but more decisively in the following decades, the idea that the inevitable decline can be curbed (perhaps even reversed in its process) with population growth is gaining ground. This thesis, which found its highest formula in Fascist and later Nazi ideology in the increase in birth rates and the protection of biological integrity through racial laws, concerns of totalitarian regimes in the face of the demographic problem highlighted. Thomas Robert Malthus had already sounded impassioned alarms in this direction, but his calculations rather predicted an unstoppable increase in population according to such a geometric proportion that the planet would not be able to bear its weight.

After World War II, between the 1950s and 1960s, the problem of an intrusive technology, which determines and disrupts man's destiny, became increasingly urgent. As a consequence of the tragedies of World War II, which had caused mourning and ruin throughout Europe, but also as a result of the atomic bombs dropped by the United States in 1945 on Hiroshima and Nagasaki, which brought the nuclear threat to the attention of public opinion, in the knowledge that such a destructive force could lead to the extermination of humanity. In the years that followed, a more widespread mistrust of science and the ideals of progress, which modernity had imposed as preeminent, began to prevail, becoming aware of man's difficulties in managing technology so advanced as to be beyond his control. Man is old-fashioned is the significant title of an essay from those years by Günther Anders, who warns of the potential dangers of atomic weaponry and judges man to be "outdated" by his own technology (Anders, 1983). The mistrust in science and, consequently, in the idea of progress, formulated by modernity, also reinforces the impression of decline.

Is it true that the West is on the way out? To this question, we would like to try to provide an answer, or rather a series of multiple answers, by extending the invitation to various personalities of culture.

A proposal to this effect was sent to Zygmunt Bauman in December 2016, and the great Polish sociologist, despite being in a precarious state of health, accepted with a hopeful "I may try." His unpublished text we are reading here is probably the last one Bauman wrote before his death on January 9, 2017, in Leeds.

He had explicitly asked his wife, Aleksandra Kania, to complete it in dialogue form and send it to us as a contribution to a debate he felt was extremely urgent. This is demonstrated by the harsh tone, very unusual for him, used to dismiss the political–economic establishment of certain countries, compared to a "huge rubbish bin" containing "all things most harrowing, painful, obtrusive, and troublesome." Hence the condemnation of neo-liberalism as a "senile disease" of classical liberalism, which also contained progressive elements (John Stuart Mill, Lord Beveridge), was expressed effectively and without hesitation. An indignant Bauman, perhaps tired of being sympathetic to human weaknesses and mistakes, determined to forcefully denounce the reactionary drift underway in various parts of the world, according to that decline observed with painful apprehension but inevitably suffered globally.

With Aleksandra Kania, she points to the persistence of Oswald Spengler's thought a century later, picking up Adorno's critique of it in a short text from 1938, "Spengler After the Decline" (later published in the collection *Prisms*, 1955). Beyond the singular botanical metaphor, according to "his general historical-philosophical concepts of plant-like growth and cultural decay," Spengler—writes Adorno—"is one of the theoreticians of extreme reaction whose critique of liberalism proved itself superior in many respects to the progressive one" (Adorno 1997: 64). And if it is highly improbable to "transform Spengler's reactionary ideas into progressive aims," it is nevertheless preferable not to underestimate their cultural, ideological, and dangerously seductive significance even today.

Bauman warns us. The final sentences of his text are significant and disturbing because they were written only a few days before his death:

> The most popular choice among the actual or aspiring strong (wo)men when it comes to casting the role of the enemy (that is, as spelled out by Eco, to the processes of self-defining, integration, and self-asserting)—indeed a fully and truly meta-choice, determining all other choices by association or derivation—is currently "THE establishment," that huge rubbish bin able to accommodate all things most harrowing, painful, obtrusive, and troublesome, and, luckily for their choosers and would-be foot soldiers, an under-defined and permanently open-ended collection of have-beens who have outlived their time and are grossly overdue to be relegated to history and recorded in its annals as an aggregate of selfish hypocrites and inept failures.
>
> In a simplified rendition: establishment stands for the repulsive, off-putting, and unprepossessing present, whereas the strong (wo)men, ready to send it to the disposal tip where it belongs, appear as guides to a new beginning, after which they who have been naught shall be all. This is that "West" which—as some of us suspect with horror, whereas some others hope for with joy—is in an advanced state of decline. And good riddance (Bauman 2018a: 49).

"So be it": it even sounds brutal. Not a viaticum, but an ominous warning of dire developments if one does not have the ability to react.

Chapter 10

LUNCH AT BAUMANS'

Food ready to eat could be found
at the family table but nowhere else:
the gathering at the common dinner
table was the last (distributive)
stage of a lengthy productive process
that started in the kitchen and even
beyond, in the family field or workshop.

Consuming Life, 2007b: 78.

In the decade (2006–2016) during which I had the pleasure of meeting and frequenting Zygmunt Bauman, especially during his trips to Italy, where he used to come frequently, there were many occasions to be together at the table, but only once did the extraordinary case of having lunch at his home, in Leeds, and being "served" by him personally occur. It happened on May 2, 2014, on the occasion of the publication of *State of Crisis*, which we had written together.

That day was a memorable one: having arrived by bus on Otley Road, a four-lane boulevard that runs from the center of Leeds to the suburbs, I got off near the junction with Lawnswood Gardens, a very green residential area surrounded by a copse. Nice sunny day (which is rare for England).

I set out to find house number 1, his address. No sign, no plaque or doorbell, just a hedge surrounding a few two-storey houses and the first, hidden by a garden overgrown with vegetation. Puzzled, I don't know what to do, yet that is the right address where Bauman lives, no doubt about it. After pacing back and forth, futilely searching for some clue, I decided to resort to an ancient yet unorthodox method: calling out loud, "Zygmunt!" Immediately, I hear his voice from the house inviting me in. I pass through the gate and make my way through the foliage, following a barely noticeable passage through the grass, I see him appear at the door together with Alexandra Kania, his second wife.

Faced with my difficulties in avoiding branches and bushes, he smiles and explains: "The garden? I don't take care of it any more. I have a gardener who costs me nothing and whose name is Charles Darwin. The natural evolution of the species."

In his living room, after a cup of coffee, he shows me the first copy of *State of Crisis*, which has just arrived from the publisher. Talking about a work in progress about the end of equality, he comments bitterly, "Equality never was." He is right. I was referring to the idea of equality that modernity had promised since the eighteenth century and which contemporary society seems to have renounced today. New projects are discussed, to be set up immediately after *State of Crisis*. Something about the decline of the politician, a topic already covered by Richard Sennett, which should be updated in relation to the advance of populism. He tells me about the topics he is working on, in particular, an essay on the "self" with Rein Raud and another in collaboration with his daughters.

Then Alexandra announces the arrival of two professors from the University of Oslo, Per Bjørn Foros and Arne Johan Vetlesen. An international meeting, Zygmunt comments, between the UK, Poland, Norway, and Italy. From the living room, we pass into the dining room, where a sumptuous table is set. Italian and French wine, "focaccia," cold meats, cheeses, fish, salads, potato croquettes, and various gravies that Bauman himself serves several times, constantly getting up to change plates and cutlery, forcing Alexandra and the rest of us to remain seated and be served. He pours generous doses of Italian red wine, extolling its qualities, and to my resistance to alcohol, he firmly insists: I cannot refuse. Of course, we talk about sociology, books, travel, life experiences, but also politics, and everyone asks my opinion on Matteo Renzi (he was then the Italian premier).

Dessert is a triumph of homemade cakes, strawberries, and cream, English cheeses (the legendary Cheddar) to be tasted on canapés, all accompanied by an abundant dose of brandy, which we discover is the famous "Baumagnac," the distillate that Zygmunt delights in producing himself. Because, in addition to sociology, there are several things he successfully devotes himself to, including cooking and photography. For a time, he even thought about going into photography professionally. We talk and drink. Per Bjørn mischievously remarks that, despite the initial rejection, I have increased my drinking. But in a good company, it happens […]

Alexandra points out that Zygmunt ate very little and drank only red wine. Followed by a good *grappa morbida* (soft brandy), as he punctuates in perfect Italian. He loves to give to others, she points out. This is a characteristic trait of his character, but also a habit of his Polish origins: being generous with guests.

When he moved to Leeds, his home became an informal meeting place for friends and colleagues, with a great sense of hospitality.

I ask to see the studio where he works. Alexandra explains that he does not like to show it to others, but for us, he will make an exception. Their working times are antithetical: Alexandra works later in the day, Zygmunt gets up very early in the morning, writes and studies for four or five hours, then has breakfast and goes out for a walk.

We go upstairs to a small room with large windows, very bright, full of books in all languages. The table is cluttered with two computers, hard disks, videos, a printer, various tools, and many photos of Janina, his first wife. On the top shelf, hidden by a portrait, is the urn with her ashes.

"She is always here with me," he observes.

The customary souvenir photos are taken, and the farewell is prepared. A long, emotional embrace. Zygmunt accompanies me into the garden, wishing that there will still be a chance to meet together in Leeds next time.

A BIOGRAPHICAL NOTE

Zygmunt Bauman, born in Poznań on November 19, 1925, left Poland at the end of the sixties, where he taught at the University of Warsaw, and moved to Tel Aviv (Israel) for a few years. In 1972, he accepted a teaching post as professor of sociology at the University of Leeds, where he settled and lived, retiring from teaching in 1990. He holds the titles of Emeritus Professor of Sociology at the Universities of Leeds and Warsaw, and in 1992, he was awarded the "European Amalfi Prize for Sociology and Social Sciences"; in 1998, he received the "Theodor Wiesengrund Adorno Award" from Frankfurt am Main, while in 2010, he was awarded, together with Alain Touraine, "Prince of Asturias Award" in the Communications and Humanities category. In 2010, in his honor, the University of Leeds set up the Bauman Institute at the School of Sociology and Social Policy.

Bauman never wrote an autobiography, but there are many scattered writings, mostly in Polish, recording memories and experiences of the highlights of his life. Izabela Wagner has skillfully collated them into a book that is necessary to get to know the sociologist of liquid modernity in depth. *My Life in Fragments* (translated by Katarzyna Bartoszyńska, Polity Press, 2023a) already expresses in its title one of the characteristics of this thinker: his fragmentary nature, confirmed by his distrust of systematic works, of general theories that seek to explain the world. His books are often complex architectures that stand on scattered essays, observations, newspaper articles, or books he had read, strung together to produce a flowing discourse. He loved synthesis and, as a serial writer, produced short texts for use in different contexts.

On closer inspection, the practice of fragmentariness stems from his life experience, the sudden shift from one culture to another, from one language to another, always an exile and never rooted in one place. Yet at ease everywhere.

In an illuminating chapter ("Who am I?"), Bauman reveals the difficulty of creating a precise identity for himself in the face of so many changes: a Jew in pre-Nazi Poland, a refugee in the Soviet Union during the conflict, a Red Army officer and then an intelligence officer. First, marginalized for his association with the communist oppressor, then suspected of disloyalty to the regime, forced to take refuge in Israel, and finally exiled to England.

For a long time, there was talk of a dark past: he was suspected of having been part of the secret service, acting against his own fellow citizens. Finally, in *My Life in Fragments*, which contains previously unpublished excerpts and letters written to his daughters, we find the answers.

After the war, Bauman joins the KBW, the section of the Polish army fighting the resistance against the Soviet invader. But he was considered "a foreign body" due to his Jewish origins and was forced to resign. In 1953, when Stalin died, he was still a convinced communist. In fact, he acknowledges that he had "matured slowly" and had freed himself of that youthful conviction late, to the point of condemning all forms of totalitarianism.

In his last notes ("Before Dusk Falls," 2016), he accuses the Slovenian philosopher Slavoj Žižek of distorting the reality of communism: "I am amazed (and angered!) by the widespread tendency today to consider Žižek a left-wing person […] Impatience and a desire to take shortcuts, and separating people into useful plants and weeds, are politically, so to speak, 'beyond the spectrum': they are equally at home—and just as legally—among the left as among the right (though, in both one and the other, at the extremes). Communism and fascism, when it came to these strategic principles, were easily able to come to an understanding; the only difference was between those who, as a result of the realization of these principles, came to fill the gulags, and those who found their way to the camps. Hitler spoke to typical German nationalism in the same way as Lenin did to the typical Russian socialism of the 'mensheviks.' […] Žižek, and even, with a little bit of effort, those who are younger than he, cannot *not know*. What we are *not allowed* not to know" (Bauman 2023: 226).

BIBLIOGRAPHY OF ZYGMUNT BAUMAN

1967–2024

(1967) "Modern Times: Modern Marxism," *Social Research*, vol. 34, n. 3, pp. 399–415 [in Peter Berger, ed., *Marxism and Sociology: Views from Eastern Europe*, Appleton-Century-Crofts, 1969, pp. 1–17].

(1972) *Between Class and Elite. The Evolution of the British Labour Movement. A Sociological Study*, Manchester: Manchester University Press.

(1973) *Culture as Praxis*, London: Routledge.

(1976a) *Socialism; the Active Utopia*, London: G. Allen & Unwin Ltd.

(1976b, 2009) *Towards a Critical Sociology. An Essay on Commonsense and Emancipation*, London: Routledge.

(1978) *Hermeneutics and Social Science: Approaches to Understanding*, London: Hutchinson.

(1982) *Memories of Class. The Pre-History and After-Life of Class*, London: Routledge.

(1985) *Stalin and the Peasant Revolution: A Case Study in the Dialectics of Master and Slave*, Leeds: University of Leeds.

(1987) *Legislators and Interpreters. On Modernity, Post-Modernity and Intellectuals*, Cambridge: Polity.

(1988a) *Exit Visas and Entry Tickets*, in *Telos*, 77.

(1988b, 2017) *Freedom*, Milton Keynes, UK: Open International Publishing Ltd.

(1989) *Modernity and the Holocaust*, Cambridge: Polity.

(1990a) *Thinking Sociologically*, with Tim May, London: Blackwell.

(1990b) *Paradoxes of Assimilation*, New Brunswick: Transaction Publishers.

(1991a) *Modernity and Ambivalence*, Cambridge: Polity.

(1991b) "Postmodernity: Chance or Menace?" Lancaster: Centre for the Study of Cultural Values.

(1992a) *Mortality, Immortality and Other Life Strategies*, Cambridge: Polity.

(1992b) *Intimations of Postmodernity*, London: Routledge.

(1993) *Postmodern Ethics*, London: Blackwell.

(1994) *Alone Again. Ethics after Certainty*, London: Demos.

(1995) *Life in Fragments. Essays in Postmodern Morality*, London: Blackwell.

(1997) *Postmodernity and its Discontents*, Cambridge: Polity.

(1998) *Globalization. The Human Consequences*, Cambridge: Polity.

(1998) *Work, Consumerism and the New Poor*, Buckingham: Open University Press.

(1999) *In Search of Politics*, Cambridge: Polity.

(2000, 2011) *Liquid Modernity*, Cambridge: Polity.

(2001a) *The Individualized Society*, Cambridge: Polity.

(2001b) *Conversation with Zygmunt Bauman*, with Keith Tester, Cambridge: Polity.

(2001c) *Community. Seeking Safety in an Insecure World*, Cambridge: Polity.

(2002) *Society Under Siege*, Cambridge: Polity.

(2003a) *Liquid Love: On the Frailty of Human Bonds*, Cambridge: Polity.

(2003b) *City of Fears, City of Hopes*, London: Goldsmith's College.

(2004a) *Wasted Lives. Modernity and its Outcasts*, Cambridge: Polity.

(2004b) *Identity: Conversations with Benedetto Vecchi*, Cambridge: Polity.

(2004c) *Europe. An Unfinished Adventure*, Cambridge: Polity.

(2005) *Liquid Life*, Cambridge: Polity.

(2006) *Liquid Fear*, Cambridge: Polity.

(2007a) *Liquid Times: Living in an Age of Uncertainty*, Cambridge: Polity.

(2007b) *Consuming Life*, Cambridge: Polity.

(2008a) *The Art of Life*, Cambridge: Polity.

(2008b) *Does Ethics Have a Chance in a World of Consumers?* Cambridge, MA, Harvard University Press.

(2009a) *Living on Borrowed Time. Conversations with Citlali Rovirosa-Madrazo*, Cambridge: Polity, 2009.

(2009b) "The Spectre of Barbarism—Then and Now," *Le Cahiers Européens de l'Imaginaire*, 1, CNRS.

(2010) *44 Letters from the Liquid Modern World*, Cambridge: Polity.

(2011a) *Collateral Damage. Social Inequalities in a Global Age*, Cambridge: Polity.

(2011b) *Culture in a Liquid Modern World*, Cambridge: Polity.

(2012a) *This is Not a Diary*, Cambridge: Polity.

(2012b) *On Education*, with Riccardo Mazzeo, Cambridge: Polity.

(2012c) *Liquid Surveillance. A Conversation*, with David Lyon, Cambridge: Polity.

(2013a) *What Use is Sociology*, with Michael H. Jacobsen e Keith Tester, Cambridge: Polity.

(2013b) *Moral Blindness,* with Leonida Donskis, Cambridge: Polity.

(2013c) *Does the Richness of the Few Benefit Us All*, Cambridge: Polity.

(2013d) *Communitas. Uguali e diversi nella società liquida*, ed. C. Bordoni. Reggio Emilia.

(2014a) *State of Crisis*, with Carlo Bordoni, Cambridge: Polity.

(2014b) *El Retorno del Péndulo*, con Gustavo Dessal, Fondo de Cultura Económica.

(2014c) "The changing nature of work and agency in times of Interregnum," *Social Europe Journal*, 9th January.

(2015a) *Of God and Man*, with Stanisław Obirek, Cambridge: Polity.

(2015b) *Practices of Selfhood*, with Rein Raud, Cambridge: Polity.

(2015c) *Management in a Liquid Modern World*, with Irena Bauman, Jerzy Kociatkiewicz, Monika Kostera, Cambridge: Polity.

(2015d) *On the World and Ourselves*, with Stanisław Obirek, Cambridge: Polity.

(2016a) *Strangers at Our Door*, Cambridge: Polity.

(2016b) *Babel* (with Ezio Mauro), Cambridge: Polity.

(2016c) *Liquid Evil*, with Leonidas Donskis, Cambridge: Polity.

(2016d) *In Praise of Literature*, with Riccardo Mazzeo, Cambridge: Polity.

(2016e) "From 'Official' to 'Do it Yourself' Fear," in *Revue Internationale de Philosophie*, ed. C. Bordoni, 3: 413–420.

(2017a) *Retrotopia*, Cambridge: Polity.

(2017b) *A Chronicle of Crisis, 2011–16*, London: Social Europe Edition.

(2017c, 2019) "Some of the Foremost Challenges to the Status Quo," in *Studia Socjologiczno-Polityczne. Seria Nowa*, 2: 31–46. Reprinted in J. J. Wiatr (ed.) *New Authoritarianism. Challenges to Democracy in the 21ˢᵗ Century. The Miracle of Reconciliation*, Leverkusen: B. Budrich, pp. 37–49.

(2018a) "That West Meant To Be Declining," with Aleksandra Kania, in C. Bordoni (ed.), *Il declino dell'Occidente revisited*. Milano-Udine: Mimesis, pp. 39–50.

(2018b) *Sketches in the Theory of Culture*, Cambridge: Polity.

(2018c) *Born Liquid*, with Thomas Leoncini, Cambridge: Polity.

(2021) *Culture and Art. Selected Writing. Vol. 1*, ed. D. Brzeziński, M. Davis, J. Palmer, Th. Campbell, Cambridge: Polity.

(2023a) *My Life in Fragments*, ed. Izabela Wagner, Cambridge: Polity.

(2023b) *History and Politics. Selected Writings. Vol. 2*, ed. M. Davis, J. Palmer, D. Brzeziński, Th. Campbell, Cambridge: Polity.

(2024) *Theory and Society. Selected Writings. Vol. 3*, ed. Th. Campbell, M. Davis, J. Palmer, D. Brzeziński, Cambridge: Polity.

Main Critical Essays on the Work of Zygmunt Bauman

Beilharz, P. (2000), *Zygmunt Bauman: Dialectic of Modernity*. London: Sage.

Beilharz, P. (2020), *Intimacy in Postmodern Times: A Friendship with Zygmunt Bauman*. Manchester: Manchester University Press.

Beilharz, P. and Wolff, J. (eds.) (2023), *The Photographs of Zygmunt Bauman*. Manchester: Manchester University Press.

Best, S. (2016), *Zygmunt Bauman: Why Good People do Bad Things*. London: Routledge.

Best, S. (2021), *Zygmunt Bauman on Education in Liquid Modernity*. London: Routledge.

Blackshaw, T. (2005), *Zygmunt Bauman*. London: Routledge.

Brzeziński, D. (2022), *Zygmunt Bauman and the Theory of Culture*. Montreal: McGill-Queen's University Press.

Davis, M. (2008), *Freedom and Consumerism. A Critique of Zygmunt Bauman's Sociology*. Aldershot: Ashgate.

Davis, M. (2013), *Liquid Sociology: Metaphor in Zygmunt Bauman's Writings on Modernity*. London: Routledge.

Davis, M. and Tester, K. (eds.) (2010), *Bauman's Challenge: Sociological Issues for the 21st Century*. Basingstoke: Palgrave Macmillan.

Jacobsen, M.H. and Poder, P. (eds.) (2008), *The Sociology of Zygmunt Bauman: Challenges and Critique*. Aldershot: Ashgate.

Jacobsen, M.H. (2012), *Liquid Modern 'Utopia'—Zygmunt Bauman on the Transformation of Utopia*. London: Routledge.

Jacobsen, M.H. (ed.) (2017), *Beyond Bauman: Critical Engagement and Creative Excursions*. London: Routledge.

Jacobsen, M.H. (ed.) (2023), *The Anthem Companion to Zygmunt Bauman*. London: Anthem Press.

Palmer, J, (2023), *Zygmunt Bauman and the West: A Sociology of Intellectual Exile*. Montreal: McGill-Queen's University Press.

Rattansi, A. (2017), *Bauman and Contemporary Sociology: A Critical Analysis*. Manchester: Manchester University Press.

Smith, D. (1999), *Zygmunt Bauman: Prophet of Postmodernity*. Cambridge: Polity.

Tester, K. (2004), *The Social Thought of Zygmunt Bauman*. Basingstoke: Palgrave Macmillan.

GENERAL BIBLIOGRAPHY

Adorno, Th.W. (1955), *Prisms*, trans. S.W. Nicholsen & S. Weber. Cambridge, MA: MIT Press 1997.

Anders, G. (1956), *Die Antiquiertheit des Menschen*. München: Beck 1983.

Arendt, H. (1963), *Eichmann in Jerusalem. A Report on the Banality of Evil*. London: Penguin 2022.

Bauman, J. (1986), *Winter in the Morning. A Young Girl's Life in the Warsaw Ghetto and Beyond*. London: Little, Brown 2002.

Bauman, J. (1988), *A Dream of Belonging. My Years in Postwar Poland*. London: Virago Press 1988.

Beck, U. (1986), *Risk Society: Towards a New Modernity*, trans. M. Ritter. London: Sage 1992.

Beck, U. (2016), *The Metamorphosis of the World. How Climate Change is Transforming our Concept of the World*. Cambridge: Polity 2016.

Beilharz, P. (2000), *The Bauman Reader*. London: Wiley Blackwell 2000.

Benjamin, W. (1962), *Illuminations*, trans. H. Zohn. New York: Schocken Books 1969.

Benjamin, W. (1996), *Selected Writings*, vol. 1. 1912–26, ed. M. Bullock and M.W. Jennings. Cambridge, MA: Belknap Harvard University Press 1996.

Berman, M. (1982), *All That is Solid Melts into Air. The Experience of Modernity*. London: Verso 2010.

Bloch, E. (1954–1959), *The Principle of Hope*, trans. N. Plaice, S. Plaice, & P. Knight. Cambridge, MA: MIT Press 1995.

Bodin, J. (1576), *On Sovereignty*, ed. J.H. Franklin. Cambridge: Cambridge University Press 1992.

Bordoni, C. (2016), *Interregnum. Beyond Liquid Modernity*. Bielefeld: Transcript Verlag 2016.

Coleridge, S.T. (1798), *The Rime of the Ancient Mariner*. London: Weidenfeld & Nicolson 2012.

Comte, A. (1875), *System of Positive Polity*, trans. J.H. Bridges. London: Continuum 2001.

Dahrendorf, R. (1968), *Essays in the Theory of Society*. London: Routledge 2022.

Debord, G. (1967), *The Society of the Spectacle*, trans. K. Knabb. Berkeley, CA: Bureau of Public Secrets 2014.

Derrida, J. (1967), *Writing and Difference*, trans. A. Bass. Chicago: Chicago University Press 2017.

Derrida, J. (1972), *Dissemination*, trans. B. Johnson. London: The Athlone Press 1981.

Durkheim, E. (1893), *The Division of Labour in Society*, trans. W.D. Halls. London: Macmillan 1984.

Durkheim, É. (1895), *The Rules of Sociological Method*, ed. S. Lukes. New York: The Free Press 2014.

Eisenstadt, S.N. (2002), *Multiple Modernities*. New Brunswick, NJ: Transaction 2002.

Fraser, N. (2022), *Cannibal Capitalism: How Our System is Devouring Democracy, Care, and the Planet—and What We can do About It*. London: Verso 2022.

Fukuyama, F. (1992), *The End of History and the Last Man*. New York: The Free Press 1992.

Gobineau, J.-A. de (1853–1854), *Essay on the Inequality of Human Races*, trans. A. Collins: Independently Publ. 2020.

Gorz, A. (1988), *Critique of Economic Reason*, trans. G. Handyside & Ch. Turner. London: Verso 1989.

Gouldner, A.W. (1970), *The Coming Crisis of Western Sociology*. New York: Basic Books 1970.

Gramsci, A. (1947), *Prison Notebooks*, ed. J.A. Buttigieg. New York: Columbia University Press 2011.

Heidegger, M. (1927), *Being and Time*, ed. D.J. Schmidt. Albany: State University of New York Press 2010.

Hobbes, Th. (1651), *Leviathan*. Oxford: Oxford University Press 2008.

Husserl, E. (1913), *Ideas Pertaining to a Pure Phenomenology and to a Phenomenological Philosophy*, trans. D.O. Dahlstrom. Cambridge, MA: Hackett 2014.

Le Bon, G. (1895), *The Crowd: A Study of the Popular Mind*, London: Loki's Publishing 2016.

Lévinas, E. (1991), *Entre Nous: Essays on Thinking-of-the-other*, trans. M.B. Smith & B. Narshav. London: Continuum 2000.

Lombroso, C. (1876), *Criminal Man*, trans. R. Gibson. Durham, CA: Duke University Press 2006.

Lukács, G. (1923), *History and Class Consciousness*, trans. R. Livingstone. London: Verso 2023.

Lukács, G. (1954), *The Destruction of Reason*, trans. P. Palmer. London: Verso 2021.

Lyotard, J.-F. (1979), *The Postmodern Condition. A Report on Knowledge*, trans. G. Bennington & B. Massumi. Manchester: Manchester University Press 1984.

Malthus, Th.-R. (1826), *Essay on the Principle of Population*, ed. R. Mayhew. London: Penguin Classics 2015.

Marcuse, H. (1964), *One-Dimensional Man: Studies in the Ideology of Advanced Industrial Society*. London: Routledge 2002.

Marx, K. (1932), *Economic and Philosophic Manuscripts of 1844*. London: Grapevine 2023.

Marx, K.-F. Engels. (1848), *The Communist Manifesto*, ed. G. Stedman. London: Penguin Classics 2002.

Montesquieu, Ch. de (1750), *The Spirit of Laws*, trans. Th. Nugent. New York: Cosimo Classics 2011.

More, Th. (1516), *Utopia*, ed. D. Baker-Smith. London: Penguin Classics 2012.

Mosse, G.L. (1966), *Nazi Culture: Intellectual, Cultural and Social Life in the Third Reich*. New York: Schocken Books 1987.

Nietzsche, F. (1887), *On the Genealogy of Morality*, ed. K. Ansell-Pearson. Cambridge: Cambridge University Press 2006.

Nietzsche, F. (1878), *Human, All Too Human*, ed. M. Faber. London: Penguin 1994.

Ong, W.J. (1982), *Orality and Literacy*. London: Routledge 1982.

Ortega y Gasset, J. (1931), *The Revolt of the Masses*. London: Norton 1994.

Pinker, S. (2012), *The Better Angels of Our Nature. Why Violence has Declined*. New York: Viking 2012.

Plato. (2018), *The Republic*, trans. T. Griffith. Cambridge: Cambridge University Press 2018.

Rifkin, J. (1995), *The End of Work: The Decline of the Global Labor Force and the Dawn of the Post-Market Era*. New York: Putnam 1997.

Rousseau, J.-J. (1762), *Emile or On Education*, trans. A. Bloom. London: Penguin 1991.

Scheler, M. (1915), *Der Genius des Kriegs und der Deutsche Krieg*. Forgotten Books 2020.

Sennett, R. (1977), *The Fall of Public Man*. London: Penguin 2003.

Shirer, W.L. (1960), *The Rise and Fall of the Third Reich*. London: Arrow Books 1991.

Sighele, S. (1891), *The Criminal Crowd and Other Writings on Mass Society*, trans. A. Robbins. Toronto: University of Toronto Press 2018.

Simmel, G. (1908), *On Individuality and Social Forms*, ed. D.N. Levine. Chicago: Chicago University Press 1972.

Simondon, G. (1989), *Psychic and Collective Individuation*, ed. D. Scott. Edinburgh: Edinburgh University Press 2014.

Spengler, O. (1918), *The Decline of the West*, trans. C.F. Atkinson. New York: Alfred A. Knopf 1926.

Spengler, O. (1919), *Prussianism and Socialism*, ed. C. Von Hoffmeister. London: Legend Books 2023.

Spinoza, B. (1670), *Theological-Political Treatise*, Cambridge: Cambridge University Press 2007.

Stuart Hughes, H. (1958), *Consciousness and Society: The Reorientation of European Social Thought*. Cambridge, MA: Harvard University Press 1958.

Tönnies, F. (1887), *Community and Civil Society*, ed. J. Harris. Cambridge: Cambridge University Press 2001.

Touraine, A. (2013), *La Fin des Sociétés*. Paris: Seuil 2013.

Touraine, A. (2015), *Nous, Sujets Humains*. Paris: Seuil 2015.

Turner, V.W. (1969), *The Ritual Process: Structure and Anti-Structure*. Chicago: Aldine 1966.

Veblen, Th. (1899), *Theory of the Leisure Class*. Oxford: Oxford University Press 2009.

Wagner, I. (2020), *Bauman. A Biography*. Cambridge: Polity 2020.

Weber, M. (1904–1905), *The Protestant Ethic and the Spirit of Capitalism*, ed. P. Baehr & G.C. Wells. London: Penguin 2002.

Weber, M. (1917), *On the Methodology of Social Sciences*, trans. E.A. Shils & H.A. Finch. Glencoe, IL: The Free Press 1949.

Weber, M. (1919), *The Vocation Lectures: "Science as a Vocation"; "Politics as a Vocation,"* ed. D. Owen & T.B. Strong. Indianapolis: Hackett 2004.

Weber, M. (1922), *Economy and Society*, ed. K. Tribe. Cambridge, MA: Harvard University Press 2019.

Wright Mills, C. (1959), *The Sociological Imagination*. Oxford: Oxford University Press 2000.

INDEX

www.ingramcontent.com/pod-product-compliance
Lightning Source LLC
Chambersburg PA
CBHW031447280326
41927CB00037B/380